An American Pilot
in the Skies of France

Percival T. Gates
(Owls Head Transportation Museum) (OHTM)

An American Pilot in the Skies of France

The Diaries and Letters of Lt. Percival T. Gates, 1917–1918

Edited by
David K. Vaughan
Air Force Institute of Technology

WRIGHT STATE UNIVERSITY, PRESS
Dayton, Ohio

Copyright © 1992 by
Wright State University Press

University Press of America®, Inc.
4720 Boston Way
Lanham, Maryland 20706

3 Henrietta Street
London WC2E 8LU England

All rights reserved
Printed in the United States of America
British Cataloging in Publication Information Available

Co-published by arrangement with
Wright State University Press

Library of Congress Cataloging-in-Publication Data

Gates, Percival T. (Percival Taylor), 1897-
An American Pilot in the Skies of France :
The Diaries and Letters of Lt. Percival T. Gates,
1917-1918 / edited by David K. Vaughan.
p. cm.
Includes bibliographical references and index.
1. Gates, Percival T. (Percival Taylor), 1897-   —Diaries.
2. Gates, Percival T. (Percival Tayor), 1897-
—Correspondence.   3. World War, 1914-1918
—Aerial operations, American.
4. World War, 1914-1918—Campaigns—France.
5. World War, 1939-1945—Personal narratives, American.
6. Air pilots, Military—United States—Biography.
7. United States. Army. Air Service—Biography.
I. Vaughan, David Kirk. II. Title.
D606.G38   1991
940.4' 4973' 092—dc20   91-26195 CIP

ISBN 1-882090-02-0 (cloth : alk. paper)

 The paper used in this publication meets the minimum requirements of
American National Standard for Information Sciences—Permanence
of Paper for Printed Library Materials, ANSI Z39.48–1984.

Contents

Preface		ix
Foreword *by Percival T. Gates, Jr.*		xi
Introduction		1

The Gates Diaries and Letters

Part 1	Pilot Training, Park Field, Millington, Tennessee (1 Jan–15 Mar 1918)	19
Part 2	Across the Ocean to Blois, France (21 May–16 Jun 1918)	35
Part 3	Flying Training, 3rd Aviation Instruction Center, Issoudun, France (17 Jun–6 Aug 1918)	53
Part 4	Gunnery School, St. Jean-de-Monts, France (7–25 Aug 1918)	105
Part 5	Ferry Pilot, Orly Field, Paris, France (26 Aug–7 Sep 1918)	127
Part 6	Assignment to the 185th Aero Squadron, Colombey-les-Belles, France (8–29 Sep 1918)	137
Part 7	Temporary Duty with the 27th Aero Squadron, Rembercourt, France (30 Sep–17 Oct 1918)	147

| Part 8 | Return to the 185th Aero Squadron; the Armistice and After (18 Oct 1918–23 Jan 1919) | 167 |

Appendices

| The Flight Log of Percival T. Gates | 189 |
| List of Names | 203 |

| Bibliography | 207 |

Index

List of Illustrations

—	Percival T. Gates	Frontis
1	The Frederick T. Gates Family	2
2	Curtiss JN4 in flight near Memphis, Tennessee	23
3	Curtiss JN4 "Jenny" in flight	24
4	The S. S. Leviathan	37
5	Map of France	47
6	Flying field at Issoudun, France	59
7	Wrecked Rouleurs, Issoudun	64
8	Percival, Alice, and Russell Gates, Tours	66
9	Nieuport 23, Issoudun	74
10	American Aviators' Cemetery, Issoudun	80
11	Aircraft destroyed by wind damage, Issoudun	85
12	Percival Gates and gunnery range, Issoudun	89
13	Image from Percival Gates' camera gun, Issoudun	92
14	Gates' wrecked Camel on the beach near St. Jean-de-Monts	116
15	Gunnery school graduating class, St. Jean-de-Monts	124
16	Percival and Alice Gates, Tours	130
17	Russell Gates and Moraine aircraft, Issoudun	145
18	Map of Front near Verdun	151

| 19 | Frank Luke and aircraft of 27th Aero Squadron | 156 |
| 20 | Captain Jerry Vasconcells and aircraft of the 185th Aero Squadron | 174 |

Preface

The diaries and letters of Lt. Percival T. Gates, written from January, 1918, to January, 1919, illuminate an important period of American history. They provide a detailed description of the life of a World War I Air Service pilot, one of the first generation of American combat pilots, as he moved from student to veteran. In addition, they provide a comprehensive account of the American Air Service flying training program in the relatively brief period of time in which it was in place in the latter part of 1918. The Gates materials give a personal view of the war in the air, a realistic description of an aspect of World War I often distorted by romantic interpretations.

Gates' diaries and letters record the step-by-step progress of a student through both the American and French flying training programs; the events described and the flight data included in his pilot's log give a comprehensive picture of aircraft, flying times, training maneuvers, and equipment used. Gates' record is especially valuable because he successfully progressed through all training schools on the road to a combat unit (and not all students completed the rigorous training program that Gates endured). His account gives a clear idea of the standard training program that was instituted by the Air Service in the months before the war ended. At the time of the war's cessation, many pilots were in the training pipeline, but few had completed their training. Gates' account of

PREFACE

accidents, injuries, and deaths in both the American and French training programs makes vividly clear the hazards of the flying training programs, illustrating the often unappreciated truth that the threat of death in combat was only the last and most publicized of dangers facing World War I pilots.

The diaries and letters, originally organized in two separate packages, have been arranged in chronological order, in the order in which they were written, with diary entries and letters intermixed. This arrangement yields a clear picture of Gates' progress through his training programs and combat units. The narrative is divided into eight sections; each section is prefaced with a short editorial introduction providing necessary continuity and explanatory details. A List of Names following the narrative gives additional information about some of the individuals mentioned in the Gates narrative when additional information has been found. In addition to the List of Names, the Appendix reproduces information found in Gates' log book. A bibliography lists additional sources describing the American flying experience in World War I.

The diaries and letters of Percival T. Gates have been donated to the Owls Head Transportation Museum, Owls Head, Maine, by Percival T. Gates, Jr., son of the author. My greatest debt is owed to him for his enthusiastic support of efforts to prepare this manuscript for publication. My thanks goes also to all members of the Gates family who have contributed supporting documentation and information.

I would like to thank the members of the Owls Head Transportation Museum for the assistance they have provided, including Charles Chiarchiaro, Director; James Rockefeller, Trustee; and Colleen Morang, Secretary. I would also like to express my appreciation to Fred Archibald, Parker Dunton, Ken Ciancette, John Crowell, and John Kincaid, all volunteer workers at the Owls Head Museum, for their contributions to the cause of aeronautical education. Just as the spirit of World War I aviation lives in the diaries and letters of Percival T. Gates, so is it also brought to life through the efforts of these individuals and the other volunteer workers at Owls Head.

Foreword

by Percival T. Gates, Jr.

We had the good fortune to grow up with a dad who was an inveterate story teller. He always found something to relate which was light, humorous, and often carried a message of importance in life. He loved to sing the old songs and to recite epic poems, some of which he'd memorized as a child. But his favorite subject involved tales of flying and his WWI adventures in France. From my earliest years I recall sitting spellbound as he told of crashes from which he'd miraculously escaped. Somehow we never tired of hearing the same escapades again and again. My childhood propensity for building model airplanes and indulging in dreams of becoming a pilot is not hard to explain.

Dad's career was in manufacturing. His first job as a banker in New York City apparently didn't challenge him. But his felt-making company provided an effective vehicle for him to express himself in innovative ways. While he never spoke of it as such, I think the daily contact with machinery, seeing raw materials magically converted into finished goods, and achieving new markets through bold new products brought him a great deal of satisfaction. Although never trained as an engineer, he had an innate feel for the properties of materials and could visualize new processes and improved machine elements. He was a fine mechanic who followed advances in automotive design with keen interest and enjoyed adjusting motorboat engines for peak performance.

FOREWORD

Our family leisure hours and mealtimes were enhanced with his sharings of business activities, stories of trips, summer vacations, and childhood adventures. He knew dozens of stories of Pat and Mike, could always recall an appropriate joke, or retell the the tale of Br'er Rabbit. He taught us to spin tops, play mumblety-peg and marbles. But when he talked of war, whether recalling a particular training flight or perhaps describing the conditions under which the first night pursuit missions were flown in France, his whole demeanor changed. He became more animated and fully engaged in these stories than I recall accompanying other topics in his life.

His military service spanned a period of less than eighteen months. But in that brief interval his experiences forged a vital aspect of his makeup that must have strongly contributed to his inner sense of wellbeing. Growing up as the youngest of seven children, in what was probably a rather authoritarian household, gave him little space in which to follow his own star. But the war provided such an opportunity and he suddenly was on his own and participating in a cause strenuously supported by his family, friends, and country. He had his first real chance to become his own person and to earn the respect and admiration of others through his skills, energies, and spirit.

In his declining years, I think he found a deep sense of meaning in the efforts he had made those many years before and he was quietly proud of his participation in the Great War. Those memories were of significant comfort to him and remained vivid as others inevitably began to fade.

On the occasion of his 80th birthday we had a memorable family celebration. As one token of our feelings we gave him a poem we'd written in his honor. Fitted to the form of a Japanese haiku and preserved as a framed illuminated calligraph, it reads:

> Caring, Courageous
> Aviator, Humorist
> Modest, Beloved:
> Dad

> Percival T. Gates, Jr.
> Rockport, Maine
> April, 1990

Introduction

Family Background

The Gates family was exceptional by any standard of measurement; Percival's father, Frederick Gates, an influential advisor to John D. Rockefeller Senior, assisted in the administration of the affairs of the Rockefeller Foundation. The six Gates children born before Percival excelled in school, business, and social work. As Percival was growing up, he found himself the junior member of a prosperous and success-oriented family; the Gates family members had established high levels of achievement. Percival Taylor Gates was born January 3rd, 1897, in Montclair, New Jersey, the seventh child of Frederick Taylor and Emma Cahoon Gates. The closest in age to Percival was his sister Grace, two years older; the eldest son, Frederick L., was eleven years older. In addition, there were two brothers, Franklin and Russell, and two sisters, Alice and Lucia. Mrs. Gates' unmarried sister, Florence Cahoon, also lived with the family (see Fig. 1).

Frederick Taylor Gates was a determined and industrious individual. He had been educated in New York state, at the University of Rochester, from which he graduated in 1877. He then prepared for the Baptist ministry at the Rochester Theological Seminary, which he completed in 1880. His first pastorate was the Fifth Avenue Baptist Church of Minneapolis, Minnesota.[1] He remained

INTRODUCTION

Fig. 1. The Frederick T. Gates family. Top row, from left: Franklin, Alice, Frederick, Jr., Lucia, Russell. Middle, from left: Mrs. Frederick T. (Emma Cahoon) Gates, Frederick T. Gates, Florence Cahoon (Mrs. Gates' sister, who lived with the family from the time of Fred's birth until the time of her own death). Bottom, from left: Percival, Grace. Picture taken about 1922. (OHTM)

as pastor there until 1888, when he resigned his position to embark on a fund-raising campaign in support of church-related education. Gates became increasingly interested in improving the quality of American education and soon established himself as authority in the field. Because he was successful in fund-raising efforts, he became known and respected for his work in this area as well.

One of the senior Gates' most significant achievements occurred in the summer of 1890, when he obtained a promise of financial assistance from John D. Rockefeller for the establishment of a new Baptist educational institution in Chicago, eventually to be known as the University of Chicago. With Rockefeller's promise of assistance, Gates was able to establish the institution on a solid financial basis. This event was a turning point in Gates' career, as he changed his professional interests from church work to philanthropic work, and it marked the beginning of his long period of association with John D. Rockefeller.

Rockefeller had from the first been impressed with Gates' personal energy and forthrightness in his negotiations to obtain support for the University of Chicago. Rockefeller was constantly beseiged by individuals seeking grants and donations; these demands occupied much of his time, and he was not able to devote the necessary attention to his business activities. He saw in Gates someone upon whom he could rely to manage his philanthropic affairs wisely and efficiently and offered Gates the opportunity to work with him, an opportunity that Gates accepted in September of 1891.[2] In addition to asking him to manage his philanthropic affairs, Rockefeller often sent Gates on errands to assess business and investment ventures, from which Gates returned with accurate and helpful advice.

Raymond Fosdick, biographer of John D. Rockefeller, Jr., has described Frederick Taylor Gates as "a dynamic figure of great intellectual power. He combined bold imagination and large horizons with driving energy and an almost photographic memory. Utterly fearless and often fiery in his words, he was a vivid, outspoken, self-revealing personality, who brought to his work not only lucidity and eloquence but gusto."[3] In the view of historian Allan Nevins, Gates possessed "the highly unusual combination of

INTRODUCTION

a man creatively interested in religion and philanthropy, and at the same time extraordinarily shrewd and farsighted in business."[4] Gates worked for Rockefeller for over twenty years, from 1891 until 1912, and was instrumental in establishing the Rockefeller Institute for Medical Research, the General Education Board, and the Rockefeller Foundation.

A practitioner of the Baptist religion, Gates was essentially of a liberal temperament. He distrusted much of the doctrinal approach of organized religion, and was especially wary of current educational methods, believing in "the transfer of emphasis from education by books to the deliberate and studied training of the senses by engaging [students] in action."[5] Gates saw through pretense and sham and did not hesitate to speak the truth as he saw it. These were some of the qualities that appealed to Rockefeller and which earned Gates the respect and admiration of some of the most important men in America. But they were qualities that could be intimidating to the youngest son in an achievement-oriented family. By the time America entered the war against Germany, Percival Taylor Gates had seen the pattern of significant accomplishments repeated in the actions of his older brothers and sisters.

Frederick, the eldest son, graduated from Yale summa cum laude in 1909 and eventually joined the medical staff of the Rockefeller Institute. Franklin, second oldest, was a tennis star at Yale, from which he graduated in 1912; he entered the banking profession. Russell, third oldest, also starred in tennis at Yale, where he graduated in 1914, and was one of the first volunteers for the Unites States Air Service. Russell attended ground school at the Georgia School of Technology (as it was called then) in August and September of 1917, where he was appointed cadet captain of his class. He was sent with one of the first group of cadets to receive flight training at Tours, France, in December of that year.[6]

All three daughters attended Dana Hall, a school for girls near Wellesley, Massachusetts. Although all were offered the opportunity to attend Vassar, they declined. During World War I all three enrolled in Red Cross courses, and the middle daughter, Alice, served in France as a YMCA volunteer from December of 1917 through October of 1918.[7] Alice Gates worked in the American

Introduction

aviation camp at Tours, where Russell Gates was stationed. A volume of selections from Alice's letters home was published in 1918 (*A Red Triangle Girl in France*); the book contained a preface by her father, who had strongly supported the work of the YMCA and Red Cross.[8]

After attending both Andover and Exeter, Percival Gates graduated from the Hill School at Pottstown, Pennsylvania, in June of 1917. Because he was under age, he obtained permission from his family to volunteer for service. Gates enlisted in the Air Service in September of 1917 and attended the Military School of Aeronautics at the Georgia School of Technology, Atlanta, Georgia, from October 25th through December 22nd. He attended pilot training at Park Field, Millington, Tennessee, from January to March of 1918. Following pilot training, he attended gunnery school at Camp Dick, near Dallas, Texas, in April. He sailed for Europe from New York City in late May, arriving in Brest, France, at the end of the month. When he arrived, he became the third of the seven Gates children to serve in France.

Gates was assigned to the 3rd Aviation Instruction Center, Issoudun, France, and was in training there during June, July, and August. At Issoudun, Gates flew a variety of Nieuport training aircraft, and graduated as a chasse (pursuit) pilot. He then attended the first class of the United States-run gunnery school at St. Jean-de-Monts, France. Then followed a two-week assignment as a ferry pilot at Orly Field, Paris, where he delivered aircraft to units in France while he awaited his assignment to a combat unit.

His initial combat assignment was to the 185th Aero Squadron, located at Colombey-les-Belles, which he joined on the 8th of September. The squadron was in the process of becoming combat-ready, and he spent most of the month of September in training. On the 30th of September he was transferred on short notice as a temporary replacement to the 27th Aero Squadron, and flew in combat with the 27th through the first three weeks of October. Gates was transferred back to the 185th Aero Squadron on the 18th of October. By that time the squadron had been assigned a night pursuit mission, and Gates participated in a number of night and day patrols until the Armistice brought a stop to combat.

INTRODUCTION

Throughout December and January Gates occupied himself with non-flying activities. He returned to the United States in February of 1919, sailing on the same ship with his brother Russell, who had completed the war as an instructor pilot at Issoudun.

After he returned, Percival returned to school, graduating from the University of Chicago in 1922. In October of that year he married Frances Crozier; three sons were born, Gregory, Percival, Jr., and Christopher. Gates eventually received a Master's Degree in Botany from the University of Wisconsin and pursued careers in banking and manufacturing. He founded the Drycor Felt Company in 1932 in Belleville, New Jersey. His company achieved commercial success as a result of his innovative ideas for making papermakers' felts. He adapted a process of using banks of barbed needles to impress wool fibers into an endless roll of basecloth material. The resulting fabric provided several improvements in performance over conventionally woven felts. In 1947 the company moved its base of operations to Staffordville, Connecticut. Although Gates did not pursue a career in flying after his return from the war, the Gates association with flying has continued; his son, Percival Gates, Jr., flew F-86s in the Korean War, and his grandson, Percival Gates III, is currently an F-16 pilot on active duty with the United States Air Force.

The World War I Air Service Flight Training Program

When the United States entered the war against Germany and its allies in April of 1917, the training program for Air Service pilots was practically non-existent. Many men volunteered for flight training, but there were few facilities and little equipment available for training. The primary Army pilot training school was located at North Island, in San Diego, California, and there was really only one other airfield of any size, at Mineola, on Long Island, New York. There were in the Air Service 130 officers, 65 of whom were flying officers of various qualifications and proficiency; a corps of just over 1000 enlisted personnel; and approximately 200 aircraft, most of them obsolescent and under-powered.[9] As one historian has said, "the United States went to war without an air force worthy of the name, and without any well formulated ideas, much less plans, for building and employing such a force in battle."[10]

Although the British and French had been actively involved in aircraft production and pilot training for over two and a half years before the United States entered the conflict, American experience in these two areas was severely limited. Thus, when the decision was made to enter the war, both aircraft and airfields were in short supply. However, by the end of 1917, less than nine months later, the number of pilot training fields available had increased from two to eighteen.[11] By the time of the armistice, the United States had established 25 flying schools in America and operated another 16 in England, France, and Italy.[12] The number of training aircraft had increased accordingly, to a total of almost 1800, though training aircraft (the Curtiss JN4D) did not appear in adequate numbers until early in 1918, nearly a year after American entry into the war.[13]

In 1917, however, the American government was faced with the problem of many volunteers to fly but no system for training them. One early solution was to send groups of cadets to training locations in England (in Tunbury and Ayr), France (Tours), and Italy (Foggia), where it was hoped that allied personnel would be able to provide aircraft and instruction. But the allies were short-handed and employed their facilities and personnel to train their own pilots. Most of the cadets who had been sent to Tours, France, in December of 1917 spent the winter in idleness, waiting for their training program to begin. Some of the cadets sent to England were able to receive training and eventually flew with British units, like the American Elliott White Springs, who flew with Billy Bishop's 85 Squadron before joining the American 147th Aero Squadron. A lesser number in Italy received training.

There was no organized training program in America throughout much of 1917; it was not until early in 1918 that the United States began to develop a training program that could accommodate the large number of student pilots necessary to fill the ranks of the Air Service aero squadrons planned for wartime operation. By the summer of 1918, a stabilized and comprehensive flying training sequence had been established. It included ground school (from eight to ten weeks), preliminary flight training (three to four months), advanced flight training (two to three months) and specialized flight training, like gunnery, bombing, or observation schools (from two to four weeks).[14]

The most important advanced flying training course was conducted at Issoudun, France. The two primary commanders of the 3rd AIC were Major Carl Spaatz, later head of the Air Force after World War II, and Colonel Hiram Bingham, who before the war had been one of Russell Gates' professors at Yale. In his post-war memoir, Bingham, commander of the Issoudun training complex from 23 August 1918 until the end of the war, stated that because "it was practically impossible during the continuance of the war for our pilots to do much more than get their preliminary training and acquire their wings before coming to France, it became necessary to develop at Issoudun a complete course in advanced flying and in aerial tactics."[15] The aircraft used at the Issoudun training center consisted primarily of outmoded Nieuport combat aircraft, whose sensitive flying characteristics were similar to those of current combat aircraft like the Nieuport 28, the Spad 13, and the Sopwith Camel.

Counting travel time (including the voyage by troop ship across the Atlantic) the entire time in training could run as long as ten months, not counting delays resulting from bad weather, shortage of equipment, sickness, or injury. The timing of this schedule meant that an Air Service pilot trainee who entered the training sequence after February of 1918 was probably still in the training pipeline when the war ended, on November 11, 1918. Although he might have received the benefit of a well-planned training program, the trained pilot was often unable to join a combat unit prior to the end of the war. According to one source, over 17,000 cadets had been sent to flying schools in the United States or overseas by the time of the Armistice; also, at the same time, there had been graduated from advanced training schools in Europe a total of 1674 fully trained American pilots.[16] Thus approximately one in ten who entered flight training in America or abroad completed all phases of training and was prepared to fly in combat in American units. This training schedule also explains why only five American flying units were ready to fly in combat by the first of June, 1918. By November 1, ten days before the armistice, 36 American units were combat-ready; the training pipeline was beginning to produce large numbers of trained aircrew members as the war ended.[17] Only those individuals who entered the Air Service in late 1917 or early 1918 were likely to have completed the recently-developed training program in time to fly in combat.

Percival Gates was one of the relatively few American pilots who were products of a reasonably stabilized Air Service flying training program and who was also able to fly in combat in the autumn of 1918. Very little has been written about this route to air combat. Most other published accounts of war flying experiences are from individuals who went through earlier, non-standard flight training programs; informative accounts of their experiences were written by Eddie Rickenbacker, Elliott White Springs, Harold Hartney, Norman Archibald, Willis Fitch, and various members of the Lafayette Escadrille and other French squadrons. While these earlier accounts are invaluable for their impressions of the war in the air, none describe the typical experiences of the representative Air Service pilot who was a product of the Air Service training system.

Another aspect of the World War I air war experience that these other accounts do not tell us much about is the awful danger of the flight training experience itself. The number of fliers killed or injured in training due to accidents, inexperience, and faulty equipment was appalling. From January to May of 1918, one hundred and three fatalities occurred in training in the United States, over twenty deaths a month.[18] The dangers of aerial combat over the front lines were in fact only the last of a series of hazardous activities that began with the first flight of pilot training. It is not generally recognized that more American fliers were killed while learning to fly in combat than were killed in aerial combat. Of over 12,000 cadets who began flight training in the United States, 204 were killed; the deaths of instructors and other personnel accounted for another 74 fatalities.[19] In flying training schools in Europe, 152 American pilots were killed.[20] Against a total of 256 training fatalities, 191 pilots were killed in action.[21] Thus, a pilot's chances of being killed while flying in training were 25 percent greater than flying in combat. If one counts the additional 74 deaths that occurred in other training accidents in the United States, the percentage of the likelihood of death in training or related flying activities as opposed to combat increases to nearly 40%.

Percival Gates's diaries document the hazards of flight training; during a three week period from 12 February to 4 March 1918 at his preliminary flight training field in Tennessee, he recorded three mid-air collisions and one ground accident, which resulted in the deaths of two instructors and six students and serious injuries to another student. While he was in training at Issoudun, France, Gates recorded the deaths of at least fifteen students and one nurse (killed while riding in a plane). According to Gates's own records, nearly twenty-five deaths occurred in his flight schools during the four months that he was in training; during the two months of his combat duty, he indicates that one pilot was killed, one was wounded, and one failed to return from a mission. It is not surprising, then, that the information in Gates' diary entries during training is as important as it is during the time that he was in combat. It is also not surprising that Gates expresses the thought that he does not expect to survive the war.

The Function of the Diaries and Letters

Both Russell and Alice Gates had arrived in France in December of 1917, and both were stationed at the 2nd Aviation Instruction Center at Tours. During the winter of 1917–18, Russell Gates was waiting restlessly for a French flight training program to begin, while Alice was busy serving in a YMCA canteen. As a YMCA worker, Alice came in contact with nearly every American aviator who trained at Tours from January through September of 1918, and the Gates family name was well-known among American aviators. Back in Montclair, New Jersey, there were two brothers, two sisters, the parents, and an aunt. Thus Percival Gates had an extensive network of family members with which he corresponded regularly. Gates wrote regularly to his sister Alice, and to his

Introduction

brother Russell. Only one of his letters to his brother has survived in this collection. He addressed a different family member in successive letters home, acknowledging each one with an appropriate comment in a letter generally intended for the entire family. Occasionally he wrote to someone outside the immediate family circle, such as his cousin Helen, whom he had met while attending gunnery school in Texas.

Gates adopted a systematic approach to accommodate the special demands of his correspondence chores. He kept a log of his correspondence to ensure that he did not inadvertently neglect one of the family members in the cycle of letters home. In addition, Gates numbered his letters so that his family could determine the order in which they were written. The combination of Gates' movements from camp to camp, the unpredictable schedule of trans-oceanic boat traffic, and the hazards of war could easily disrupt the flow of mail; the total time required to complete the communications loop amounted to six or seven weeks.

Gates' materials illustrate the importance of the diary as a necessary component of the correspondence activity. The diary provided a record of key events of the day. There were periods of time when he regularly recorded the day's events, and there were periods of time when he apparently neglected his diary in favor of letters home, or when training or combat activities kept him busy. Gates' longest continuous run of daily entries is 43 days, from the 2nd of August through the 13th of September. Then comes a gap of seventeen days, followed by a run of 16 entries in 17 days, at the end of which time (18 October), he ceased writing in his diary for the remainder of his time in France, a period of three and a half months.

Gates' diary entries provided a brief history of events and emotions; because he was not able to write home every day, and because events in his flight training program and, later, combat, often occurred at a rapid pace, his diary provided a ready reference for sorting out his experiences. His diary also became a permanent record of important details—names, places, numbers, aircraft, units, and so forth, that censorship laws prevented him from describing in his letters home. In his letters home he was often required to refer to places and units in a code that he hoped his family could decipher, adding that he would be able to provide the full story of an important event when he returned home and could fill in the details through reference to his diary. For example, he wanted very badly to tell his family about the exciting moments when his ship maneuvered violently to avoid German submarines as it was entering the harbor at Brest, but his censorship requirements reduced the episode in his next letter home to two short sentences: "The last day of our trip was most exciting. I cannot tell you about it, but I have it in my diary."

His diary served as a repository for both private fears and public meditations. Gates himself acknowledges and mocks the larger purpose of his diary in an amusing comment to his family written on the eighth of July: "I am keeping up my diary right along. Judging from the proportions it has already taken, I will have a six-volume edition for sale at the end of the war—"My Four Months in France"—you see I expect the war to quit in four months. By that time the Kaiser will know I am here and will give up."

Some incidents are recorded in the diary which are not included in letters home; these include aircraft incidents and accidents in which Gates was involved. He described only the combat crashes in his letters home (minimizing the hazards associated with them). Nor did he mention in his letters the fatalities and injuries which were occurring frequently in his training program.

Because Gates came from a family with a strong moral ethic, he was concerned to reassure his family that his stay in France was not leading him into undesirable personal behavior, and he was at pains to account for his avoidance of drink, tobacco, gambling, and other greater or lesser failings. He initially undertook a monthly summing-up of aspects of his moral and physical health, which he insisted were consistently good, as they most certainly were. He refers to his first letter to his father on the subject, dated 31 July, as his "big summary report on my mental, moral, and physical condition." He intermittently provided similar reports, usually directed to his father, throughout his stay. After the war ended, he continued to report on his fitness up to the time of his departure.

Introduction

The soldier's motivation and attitude towards the war typically followed a pattern of high initial motivation followed by gradual disillusion and increasing anxiety. Gates' letters home reveal this pattern, but because he was in a combat area for a relatively brief time (six months in France, of which less than three were devoted to active combat flying duty), his signs of disillusion and anxiety are less pronounced than those of English or French fliers, who might have seen as much as four years of high-risk combat life (if they survived). The war did have an effect on Gates; in a letter to his father dated 4 November, after one of his squadron mates failed to return from a mission, he provides instructions about his personal finances and describes what would happen to his personal effects "in case of accident." His diary also records evidence of signs of increasing anxieties eventually displayed by most pilots, including sleeplessness and modified eating habits.

The tone of his letters never becomes moody or somber; he continued to view his flying adventures and misadventures as part of the challenges of the flying life that his line of work naturally brought, and he continued to take seriously his role as responsible family representative in an important international event. Although his fellow pilots teased him about his strict moral stand, it is also clear that they respected his beliefs and his proven reliability as an aggressive and motivated pilot.

One of the crucial aspects of Gates' communication ethic is the sense of purpose he carried with him as spokesman as well as participant in a combat environment. Gates saw himself not merely as a recorder of the events around him, but as an interpreter, evaluator, and transmitter of those events. He represented his family members as well as his country; he was responsible to them for the quality of his professional and personal behavior and for the accurate transmission to his family of the faithful record of that performance. His role as family representative and family historian undoubtedly gave him a sense of purpose and continuance that helped to sustain him in a struggle from which less motivated individuals did not always return.

The effect of the Gates materials results from their cumulative impact; the importance of simple events grows as subsequent events

INTRODUCTION

are described. The mere facts of history, the names, places, and dates, lend a credibility and suspense to the story equalling or surpassing a fictional approach. The momentum of the story builds continually, within each section, and from section to section; even the post-Armistice events add to the full meaning of the narrative. The entire story is an ever-developing drama. While much of the dramatic effect of the description is due to Gates' actual progress through America and France, that dramatic effect would not be successful without the descriptive powers of the writer.

Lieutenant Percival Gates was an outstanding representative of the type of individual America believed it was sending to fight for the Allied cause in France. As depicted in the diaries and letters, the nature of the narrator is open, fresh, and direct. Neither in the letters nor in the diary is there ever any sense in which the narrator is deceiving himself or his family. He is never self-righteous in his periodic moral assessments; although occasionally opinionated, Gates is never a prude, and in fact often demonstrates a self-deprecating sense of humor. As a World War I United States Air Service aviator, Percival T. Gates was truly an exceptional individual—a patriotic American, a skilled pilot, and a motivated soldier. Most importantly, he was also a survivor.

The Percival Taylor Gates collection consists of 106 separate diary entries (in two separate diaries) and 72 letters to family members (in two bound notebooks) covering the period 1 January 1918 through 23 January 1919. Additional materials include Gates' ground school notebooks, his pilot's log, and approximately 100 photographs. The text of the diaries and letters appears here essentially as it was written. Misspellings have been silently corrected, abbreviations have been expanded, and punctuation has been added when necessary for clarity. Parenthetical comments are Gates' own; editorial comments or explanations have been placed in brackets. Where additional information has been found pertaining to names mentioned in the text, those names have been marked with an asterisk (*), and a more detailed account has been placed in a List of Names in the appendix. Introductory sections precede each of the eight major divisions of the text. In general, explanatory comments have been kept to a minimum.

Introduction

Notes

1. Frederick Taylor Gates, *Chapters In My Life* (New York: The Free Press, 1977), p. 77.
2. Gates, p. 159.
3. Raymond B. Fosdick, *John D. Rockefeller, Jr.: A Portrait* (New York: Harper & Brothers, 1956), p. 83.
4. Allan Nevins, "The Man Who Gave Away Rockefeller's Millions: The Memoirs of Frederick T. Gates," *American Heritage* 6 (April 1955), p. 66.
5. Gates, p. 134.
6. Gates, pp. 147–51.
7. Gates, pp. 154–5.
8. [Alice Gates], *A Red Triangle Girl in France* (New York: Doran, 1918).
9. Col. Edgar S. Gorrell, *The Measure of America's World War Aeronautical Effort* (Norwich NH: Norwich University, 1940), p. 2.
10. Mauer Mauer, ed., The *U. S. Air Service in World War I.* 4 vols. (Washington DC: Government Printing Office, 1979). Vol 2, p. 101.
11. Arthur Sweetser, *The American Air Service* (New York: Appleton, 1919), p. 107; Gorrell, p. 12.
12. Gorrell, p. 11.
13. Sweetser, p. 263.
14. Sweetser, pp. 114–9.
15. Lt. Col. Hiram Bingham, *An Explorer in the Air Service* (New Haven: Yale UP, 1920), p. 126.
16. Gorrell, pp. 14, 22.
17. Gorrell, pp. 30–1.
18. Sweetser, p. 123.
19. Sweetser, pp. 263, 268.
20. Gorrell, p. 15.
21. Gorrell, p. 64.

THE GATES DIARIES AND LETTERS

PART 1

Flight Training, Park Field, Millington, Tennessee, 1 January to 15 March 1918

[Gates attended the School of Military Aeronautics at the Georgia School of Technology from October 25 to December 22, 1917. The topics listed in his course of study included military studies, signalling, gunnery, aids to flight, airplanes, engines, and aerial observation. Gates received good grades in all subjects; his highest marks were earned in gunnery, airplanes, and engines. After a short, one-week Christmas vacation with his family in New Jersey, Gates returned to Georgia Tech for assignment to a flying school. He was assigned to Park Field, Millington, Tennessee, located a few miles north of Memphis. The flying school had recently been established, on December 1st, and he and many of the students were initially housed in tents.

Gates was assigned to Park Field from January 7th through March 15th of 1918. He first flew on the 10th of January and was cleared to fly solo on February 15th, Valentine's Day. His course of flight instruction was hampered by winter weather and numerous casualties. During a three week period in February and March, six students and two instructors were killed in four flying accidents, of which Gates personally witnessed two. He was asked to identify the body of one student whom he had known well. The sight of his dead friend disturbed him for some time; as he says in his diary, "the thought of poor old Jimmy came back to me in spite of everything." He himself was involved in an aircraft incident on the day of his first solo flight.

Gates' description of flying activities graphically illustrates the hazards of flight training at Park Field; during one flying period on 30 January, he records six aircraft accidents: a wheel breaks loose from one aircraft, another aircraft goes up on its nose on landing, and four others experience broken propellors. Later another aircraft catches fire and flips over on its back while landing. The large number of accidents which occurred at Park Field and other training bases in the early months of 1918 was due largely to Air Service inexperience in conducting training programs of such magnitude. The accident rate dropped after regularized training procedures were established.

Gates' log book shows that he flew thirty-eight training flights at Park Field, about twenty of which he flew solo, in the Curtiss "Jenny." He accumulated a total of thirty-two hours and forty-seven minutes of flight time. The average altitude he reached in the fourteen flights he made before being cleared for solo was 500 feet. The highest altitude he reached during flight school was 4000 feet. Most of his solo work at Park Field consisted of figure eights, spirals, and a few stalls, slips, and spins. He completed his course with the required cross-country navigation flight, which included an unscheduled forced landing due to engine trouble.]

Tuesday, January 1, 1918: I started for Atlanta today to get my assignment to a Flying Ground [training field]. The train to Washington was jam full so that I had to stand as far as Philadelphia. At Washington I had a long wait for my train, but they finally got it made up.

Wednesday, January 2: It is snowing hard this morning and apparently all the water supplies of the railroad are frozen up as we have no water on the train. Traveling certainly is hard and tiresome. I got off at Charlotte to visit the Drapers. Mr. Draper met me at the station and took me up to his home where I found Mrs. Draper, Joy, Billy, and three guests. The afternoon was very quiet as both Joy and I were not feeling well. Joy had just had the grippe while I was breaking out with Indigestion. We had a long talk about the war.

Thursday, January 3: This is my birthday. 21 at last. We spent the morning talking, reading, and playing pool. This rest certainly was a lucky thing as I am not feeling well and have a cold trying to get a hold. I took my train for Atlanta at three-thirty. While waiting in the station a military funeral passed by. Those poor fellows in the draft camps are getting it pretty hard. A good many die every week from pneumonia. The cold weather with no equipment is terrible. I met Potts, Buchanan, and Rothfield on the train. The train must have been too big for the engine as we kept stopping all the time and finally got here at Atlanta at 2:30 AM. We got a little to eat and a good room at the Piedmont.

Saturday, January 5: I slept till noon yesterday and then reported out at school. However, I could not get any dope so I was ordered to report again this morning. I called on Peggy Mitchell* in the afternoon and had a good time. She seemed to be quite grieved over the fact that I was going the next day. In the evening I went to the Lyric with Mr., Mrs., and Lois Lottridge* and some friends including Mrs. Slaughter*. The show was rotten but the company was fine. This morning I got up early to report at Tech by eight o'clock. After getting straightened out I went over to Courteney Ross's for dinner. I had a good time but I did not get away as well as I hoped. The candy I sent her this evening may help. I spent most of the evening getting my trunk and repacking it at the baggage room. I watched a big crap game but did not join it.

Tuesday, January 8: We started from Atlanta Sunday morning (the sixth) at about seven o'clock. We reached Birmingham at two o'clock, too late for our connection to Memphis. We stayed over at

Birmingham till 11:45 that evening. During that time I took in one movie in the afternoon with Cook, Johnson, and Dudley. After the show we met a young fellow who tried very hard to get us to stay at his house for dinner (nothing doing). We passed a carload of girls and endeavored in vain to pick them up. They passed us about six times but they would not stop. In the evening I went to a movie with Webb who insisted on picking up a couple of women but I was not in on that. We took the train at about nine o'clock and went to bed.

The next morning, that was yesterday, we got to Memphis too late to get our train to Millington. We stayed at Memphis until we were taken in by two Army trucks. The ride out was mighty hard on the rear as there were apparently no springs on the truck. As we approached the field we could see the planes circling around in large circles and landing on the field. It certainly was a great sight [Fig. 2]. After we got signed up we were put in one of the class rooms and issued our stuff: real spring beds, mattresses, pillows, blankets, and a comforter. After the barracks were fixed up, we were off to watch the flying, write letters, etc.

This morning we started in at 5:15 with the moon shining bright. Then there was nothing till breakfast, except letter writing and watching the flying. At 8:00 we reported for trap shooting until 10:00 when we had a class in machine gun. The machine gun primarily consisted in pointing out different names for parts we had had before. After dinner we were off except for moving a stove which did not take long. I have just come back from a general cussing out to the entire school for insubordination to non-commissioned officers.

Friday, January 11: Had not much time to write up this thing before so I will write it up now. On the 9th we had trap shooting in the morning and classes in the afternoon. I went on a detail instead and got stuck oiling the floor for A barracks. It certainly was a dirty job. We started engine and airplane lectures in the evening. Yesterday I got my first ride and it certainly was great. The first trip was rather tame but the second was a peach. We had a fellow named Frye with a Curtiss JN4D joy stick control [Fig. 3].

Pilot Training

Fig. 2. Curtiss JN4 in flight near Memphis, Tennessee. (United States Air Force) (USAF)

Fig. 3. Curtiss JN4 "Jenny" in Flight (USAF)

Pilot Training

He took me up and did a few dips that almost put me to sleep. Then he climbed to 4000 feet and turned some [figure] 8s. Coming out of the turn was a great sensation, a combination of rising and turning. I never felt anything like it before. Then he took me down in a sharp 90 degree bank spiral. That certainly was some ride.

In the afternoon we worked in the hangars and on the buzzer [Morse Code]. It started to hail in the evening and continued all night. It snowed hard all the morning so that there was no flying. We had hangar work instead. This afternoon we had I. D. R. [military drill practice] and buzzer. This has been a poor day, nothing doing but work in dry classes. The buzzer is the only thing that is of much value. More engines and airplanes tonight.

Sunday, January 13:   We did not have anything yesterday morning except work in the hangar setting up machines. It was about the coldest day I ever saw down here. It started out eight below zero. In the afternoon we had aerial observation by Captain Giddings. He gave us a great cussing out for having leather coats and "swanking" too much. He then proceeded to tell what he had done. He brought down twelve German planes and had lived longer than any other aviator at the front. He had been given all the medals he could get. Later we had buzzer.

We all took the train for Memphis at 3:15. We [were going] to the Chilison [Hotel] for dinner but [the train] did not get there in time so we (Cook and I) did not wait. We went to a show in the evening and had supper after it. I had a room with Dudley and Johnson. Johnson did not come in until *late* and I had to sleep with him. We did not get up until noon. Then I went to a show with Webb and looked around but no one would pick us up or take us in. I took the train this evening from Memphis and got to Millington late and dark. The snow was deep and the walking was hard. I almost got hit going past the guard. I slipped while passing him and he thought I was going for his gun. This evening I wrote a couple of letters.

Tuesday, January 15:   It rained all day yesterday. The result was slush about a foot thick. We had to wade up to Hangar 11 but outside of that we did not get so wet. I wrote a bunch of letters and got a peach from Courteney thanking me for some candy I sent her. I wish I knew her better as she is a peach. I spend most of my time here writing in hopes of getting a few replies. Letters are the mainstay of life around here on bad days. Today it was clear but still too much snow for any flying.

I wrote a lot more letters and got one from Peggy [Mitchell]. She tried to kid me about my opinion on war marriages (a rather delicate subject) but I think she got bit worse than I did. It is funny what an effect this Army life has on one. It makes me feel real "devilish" with the ladies. I guess it is due to the fact that I don't see any. I make a fool of myself whenever I talk to a girl. However, I have got will power enough to keep straight which is more than most of the fellows do. So long as my fun is innocent I guess it will be all right. When I see this "stuff" that goes on all around me, I wonder if I will be able to come out with a clean record. Pray God I will, "For there are those who care." I got a wonderful letter from Fred today that helps. I was on KP this afternoon from four to eight. It was pretty good fun and I got a *good* meal out of it.

Sunday, January 20: Everything has gone on as usual since I wrote this up last. The only thing out of the ordinary is that we started to fly yesterday but the snow came down so fast we had to stop. It turned into a regular blizzard finally and lasted all day. We moved out into these little huts Friday. They aren't so bad with wooden floors, sides built up six feet, and a stove in the middle. That is some stove too. It is just a big funnel set upside down with a chimney on top and a hole cut in the side to stoke it up. Cook, Dudley, Strahan, Cunningham, Johnson, Reid, and Williams are living with me. We get along finely.

Strahan and I are here alone over Sunday and we spend most of our time writing letters. I made out a record of my correspondence so I will be able to keep track of my letters. We had our examination in engines and another in airplanes yesterday. I think I passed them as they weren't very hard. There has been a great change in the mess lately. A new board has taken it up and has done wonders.

Pilot Training

Friday, January 25: It has been some time since I have written this thing up but nothing special has gone on. I managed to pass the engines and airplane exams with 98. We did not do much of anything Monday or Tuesday except in the last afternoon when we took a walk. They started flying in the afternoon but the snow was pretty thick—

Sunday, January 27: I had to stop in the middle of writing this up to go to class. Wednesday the cadets started flying. Class A flew in the morning but most of the machines froze up. We flew in the afternoon and spent most of our time keeping her level and making landings—that is some job. I did very poorly and was pretty discouraged. Thursday Class B flew in the morning. That was great work. I got in an hour flying, ending up with a little joyride at the end. I did a lot better though I still had a tendency to give up the controls as we neared the ground. In the afternoon we had to move the dugouts. Every one had to be put on a new foundation and turned around. We finished about four of them by eight at night. My feet were wet all day and as a result I got considerable of a cold.

Friday the weather was warm and the flying poor. We had machine gun and trap shooting in the morning. In the afternoon we flew. I spent my time making landings but the others made 8s. Saturday it was very misty and Duryea was the only one to fly. They had to call it all off on account of the fog. We had a couple of classes in the afternoon and an inspection. In the evening we had a dance. I took Clare Dunscombe. I had a pretty good time but there wasn't enough cutting in. Clare was [a] mighty nice girl. I slept till two o'clock Sunday and then went to a show. There wasn't much going on till I got home and found a letter from Courteney—she is a peach. She sent a little picture in the letter which looks pretty good to me.

Monday, January 28: I flew again this morning but it wasn't very good. The ground was so soft that the machines kept breaking through the crust of ice. One machine went up on its nose while trying to taxi. There weren't many classes so I managed to get most of my letters written. Johnson and Dudley have been wrestling again tonight. This time Dudley got a bloody nose and bled in Johnson's eye.

Wednesday, January 30: We moved out of our little dugouts Tuesday morning the first thing. Now we are settled in Barracks No. 1. It isn't a bad place but there are some things that are not so good. There are so many of us that there isn't a chance to get any quiet or peace. Also you can't get it as hot as we could the good old tents. Between the music and the typewriters and the crap games, it is a pretty disconcerting place. In the afternoon yesterday I was due to fly but Lieutenant Frye was on guard [duty] so we stood around all afternoon.

We had a good chance to see everything that happened on the field. It was just a common day so I will describe some of the events. When we marched out we found all the machines lined up with the propellers turning slowly, just warming up. The instructors stood in a little group near the center gas house. After reporting, the different classes reported to their instructors. Then the machines began to go up, one after another. First they tested the motors with two fellows holding down each wing. Then they started off.

The field was divided into two parts, A and B. All the machines in A rose slowly off the ground one by one and circled around to the right. Those in B turned to the left. They made a circle and glided back into the field. The air was filled with machines. If it had not been for the systematic turning there certainly would be a lot of accidents. Pretty soon a machine came down with too hard a bump and one wheel gave way. Then the motorcycles followed by a truck ran out across the field. It certainly was funny to see those little motorcycles with their sidecars bouncing around along the field. One driver fell off his machine and the motorcycle balanced by the sidecar kept on going.

Another airplane came down and lit in about two feet of water. The wheels stuck and the machine went up on its nose with the tail sticking right up. Four machines broke their propellers and had to be towed in. Finally the flying began to slow up, the roar of engines began to quiet down, and the machines began to line up again. The flying was over for the afternoon.

This morning I was flying again but I was rotten. Everything seemed to go wrong. It was mostly due to the bad turn we had to make to get into the field. One machine caught fire and was forced to land. It hit in a lake covered with thin ice and turned over on its back. Mother's box of goodies, helmet, goggles, sweater, gloves, etc came today. I certainly have been waiting for it a long time, almost two weeks. No other particular news today so I will go to bed.

Wednesday, February 6: It is just a week since I have written in this thing so the following dope probably won't be very accurate. We flew most all last week but the principal event was the weekend. I went to a dance Saturday night at somebody's house and had a peach of a time. There were a bunch of officers there but they were mighty nice about it. I met Miss Mary Hamer there. She is *some* pretty girl, and mighty nice too. I stayed at the dance so long I missed the last car home but that did not bother [me] much. I got a ride home with Cunningham. Sunday I went to dinner with Slim and Dudley at Mrs. Craft's house. After dinner we went into town to the Khaki Club tea. I did not get out of there till about four thirty but there were some mighty nice people there. Then I called up Mary Hamer and went out to see her. She was as nice as I thought her at first. She can play the piano like a streak and is a mighty interesting talker. She has a couple of brothers in the Army. I did not leave her home until pretty late.

We flew on Monday and Tuesday [the 4th and 5th of February]. Then it began to thaw out and the mud was so thick we had to stop flying. We spent the rest of the week in the hangars working on the airplanes. Sunday I went to a dinner party at Clare Dunscombe's. I had a fine time and met a lot more girls. Afterwards I went out to see Mary again and had a mighty nice visit.

Tuesday, February 12: Yesterday, Monday, we started flying again. The field was pretty soft but it was drying out fast. Today has been a *black* day. It rained hard last night and early this morning but we flew just the same as the field was quite hard. Cunningham and I hid in a big box in a hangar to escape working on ships. Some fellows nailed us in the box. Finally we got out just in time for flying. I waited around for a good many hours but did not go up.

This afternoon we worked on the machine gun range. While I was getting water two machines collided in the air. They both fell heavily and both men were *killed*. They were two soloists, Rodgers and Cooley. I knew Rodgers back at Georgia Tech. Rodgers' machine struck the tail of Cooley's plane. Cooley dropped in a nose dive landing on his back. Rodgers almost recovered from the nose dive he got into as a result of striking the other machine. It was a pretty heavy shock to us all as these two boys are the first that have been killed on this field. However, the spirit is picking up again. It is all in the game. We will all get our turn sooner or later. I think it is the general opinion of most of the fellows that we won't get through the war. At least most of us. When my day comes I hope it comes the same way. Those boys were instantly killed. There was another slight accident when two other planes ran into each other. They were so low though that it did not amount to much. That is about enough for one day.

Monday, February 18: It has been some time since I wrote this up last but I don't think I am likely to forget what took place last week. We had some fine flying Wednesday. Thursday it was too windy and we could not go up. Friday was the big day though. I was first up and after going around a couple of times Lieutenant Frye got out and pretended to clean his goggles. When I was not looking he tied the good old white handkerchief to the rudder. That was the sign that I was to *solo*—February 15, Valentine's Day. I never will forget that first trip.

I was scared green until I gave her the gun. Then I got a good take off and that put confidence in me. I went on around the field just as usual, and came down on a slow glide. I hit with considerable of a bump and gave her the gun again. My next landing was pretty good. Then I went on around landing for 40 minutes. That afternoon I flew for 50 minutes more. I got a bad start though. When I took my ship out on the line, another one came down and lit on my wing. However, I got another machine and got off all right. Saturday I got in another hour's flying. But it was a bad afternoon and I did not get much out of it.

That evening I got into the city in a machine. I just fooled around that evening, got a leather coat and went to a show. Duryea had a girl to the show and I had a pretty good time. Sunday I tried to get out to see Clare and Mary but they weren't home. Today, Monday, I had a good afternoon flying but the wind was too strong for my sights. I got lost in a cloud for a couple of minutes but as I got scared I came out in a hurry.

Tuesday, February 19: There was nothing at all doing today. It rained up until late and so we did not do a thing.

Tuesday, February 26: I get to write in this thing about once a week. We had good flying Wednesday, Thursday, and Friday last week. I had a fine 75 minutes Friday. For the first time I had to reverse my controls on the 8s.

Saturday it was foggy at first so nobody flew much until afternoon. Then the dualists went up and some cross country men. About four in the afternoon I went out on the field. Just as I got there someone pointed over the hangars. There was a terrible crash and I looked around just in time to see two planes disappear nose down behind the hangars. I went to the entrance of the field and the two planes were wrecked out in the field beyond. We could not go out there so we went to the hospital to find out who was killed. They took three men out of the ambulance and put them in a little house behind the hospital. Hancock and I went over to ask who the fellows were. As the officer did not know, they asked us in to see if we could recognize them. We went in and there was Jimmy Webb the first one. His face was not cut much but it was very badly bruised. I did not know the other two men but they turned out to be Cadet Grey and Instructor Reigle. All three of the bodies were badly mangled. Just held together by their clothes. That accident certainly took the pep out of us all for a while. Fortunately we did not have to fly.

I went to the cadet dance that night to try to get the whole thing off my mind. I had a pretty good time but the thought of poor old Jimmy came back to me in spite of anything. Sunday it was better. I went out to see Mary Pickett and later Mary Hamer. I had a good time at both places.

Monday we had almost regained our old pep. There was a very strong wind in the morning. Many of the instructors complained about flying. Thronson went up once, then came down and said it was too rough. They sent him up again and again he complained that it was *too rough* for *flying*. However, they would not call it off so he went up again. On his third turn, into the wind, he got in a side slip and could not get out in time. The machine crashed to the ground near the last barracks. Both Thronson and his pupil Hanley were pretty well cut up. Thronson was unconscious. His legs were broken and he had internal injuries. He died in the evening. That certainly hit us hard. The instructor was well-liked and a good flier.

Tuesday (today) it is a fine, clear, still day. All our pep is back. We are kidding each other about whether we are due next or not. It seems funny, when you think of it, to hear the fellows put up their coats that they will come back. If one fellow gets killed the other is supposed to get his coat. I am to fly this afternoon and I must say I am crazy to get at it again.

Monday, March 4: It has been almost a week since I wrote in this last. I notice that I wrote Tuesday morning and everything was bright. Tuesday afternoon I went up to do some eights. I got into such bad side slips that I was most scared to death. I came down and a civilian instructor went up with me to show me how to do it. We made a few eights and then came down. When I got down I found that Bill Story and a fellow named Wisinger had collided and were not expected to live. Both boys died that evening. I was certainly sorry to see poor old Bill go. He was a mighty fine fellow.

That about ended the regular flying for that week. We did not get any more work in till Saturday. In the meantime the officers were working their heads off to get some rules that would prevent accidents. Saturday we got in some pretty good times. I had a wonderful time doing eights. However, I had a bad time with landings and pretty nearly got put off. They say I had the Major cussing at one time. In the evening I went into Memphis in a car and as usual I had a puncture. Saturday night I went to a show and had a pretty good time. That night I got some kind of poisoning from the sheets and could not sleep till almost 5 AM. I went to sleep for an hour in the bath tub. I made up for it Sunday though. Monday it was too windy and misty to fly. Also the civilian instructor would not fly with the cadets.

Monday, March 11: We flew a lot [on Tuesday, the 5th] and I got transferred from first to second solo class. It was pretty windy but I managed to get away with it all right. Wednesday I reported at Woodstock [an auxiliary field] for second solo and put in 85 minutes learning the country and doing eights. Thursday I went out again and did some steep eights. Friday was the same only I did some spirals that were about as tight as they could be. I almost got into a tail spin. Saturday I put in two and a half hours in the roughest weather I was ever in. I went to Memphis to kill time and almost got lost coming back. That evening I went to Memphis and did errands. Sunday I got up early and spent from 10 AM to 1:45 PM at the dentist's. That was some job. In the afternoon I went to a show with Slim and later calling.

Today, Monday, I got into trouble. I was supposed to be transferred to cross-country and stunts but as I was not I transferred myself thinking it was a mistake. I tried to find out about it from the flying office but they said to go on. I went up for 30 minutes' instruction in tail spins, stunts, and side slips. Then I went up and practiced stunts and side slips myself. They were mighty good fun. This afternoon I took two cross-country trips, one from here to Arlington and over to Memphis. The other was from here to Memphis and over to Colliersville. I did not get back until 6:20 this evening. At night I got called over to the flying office and got a calling down by Lt. Dawson for cutting his class. I don't know what will come of it but it looks pretty serious.

[Apparently nothing serious resulted from Gates' failure to attend the class. Though his diary entries end prior to the conclusion of the course, his logbook indicates that he satisfactorily completed the cross country and altitude flight portions of the course. Gates experienced engine failure during his cross-country flight, a common occurrence, because the Jenny engine, the OX-5, was notoriously unreliable.]

PART 2

Across the Atlantic to Blois

[After completing flight training at Park Field, Gates attended gunnery school at Camp Dick, Texas, located just northwest of Dallas. The course was of four weeks' duration and consisted of classroom instruction and practice firing from moving seats to moving targets, both affixed to rails. No aerial gunnery was practiced at this time, primarily because there was a shortage of training aircraft. No indication of his success at Camp Dick exists in his papers, but given his above-average gunnery scores at Issoudun and St. Jean-de-Monts, he probably earned high marks.

In April, Gates returned to New Jersey for another brief reunion with his family. He was then alerted for transfer to France. He departed New York City on the *Leviathan*, formerly the German luxury liner *Vaterland*, which had been confiscated by American authorities after the United States entered the war. Gates' diary entries resume with his account of his voyage across the Atlantic, which for most American soldiers was their first ocean-going experience, and which marked the beginning of their "Great Adventure." The *Leviathan* departed New York on the 22nd of May and arrived in Brest, France, on the 30th, after an exciting encounter with a German submarine just outside the Brest harbor. On the voyage across Gates met a young Red Cross nurse, Bernadine Fennelly, with whom he formed an ongoing friendship during his stay in France. After a five-day delay in Brest, he traveled to the

American distribution center in Blois, where he remained for nine days before receiving orders to Issoudun. While traveling from Brest to Blois he was able to visit his sister and brother at Tours. His sister Alice was a YMCA worker, and his brother Russell had just begun flight training at the 2nd Aviation Instruction Center there. During his stay in Blois he entertained himself by undertaking a vigorous schedule of visits to nearby towns and chateaux, taking advantage of the delay to further educate himself about the country and the people whose values he was committed to defend.]

Thursday, May 23, 1918: At last my dream for the past two years has come true. I am actually crossing the ocean to France, to fight "over there." All the officers were ordered on board at 10 AM Tuesday the 21st of May. We were to sail on Ship No. 22. I am actually on the *Leviathan*, the old *Vaterland*, the largest ship afloat [Fig. 4]. All day, the 21st, troops poured into the side of the ship and down into the steerage. Thirteen thousand in all, I believe, not counting the officers and ship's crew which would bring our load up to near fifteen thousand. Out in front the derricks were loading in blanket rolls, trunks, guns, ammunition in small quantities, and all kinds of field equipment. It is astonishing what a company has to take with it. About four o'clock 150 Red Cross nurses came aboard. They help a lot in passing the time as they are quite free to talk with anyone.

The ship itself is a wonderful piece of work. It appears that the Huns built the thing with the distinct idea in view of turning it into a transport when it should become necessary. All the partitions that had to be taken out were made of wood and there were no steel girders to block the way. The upper part of the boat is about the same as when it was used for a passenger ship, I imagine, except that there have been some changes made in the center section of the upper deck and A deck where the sailors live. B, C, and D decks are used for officers. The staterooms are just the same as ever with one extra bed. We have the regular beds, sheets, mattress and

Across The Ocean

Fig. 4. The S. S. Leviathan (National Archives)

blankets, ventilators, fans, running water, electric lights, etc. In fact it is just like a pleasure voyage for all the officers and nurses.

It is quite different for the poor doughboys, however. They live down below in little steel beds piled one on top of the other with about 18 inches between the top of one and the bottom of the other. I do not see how the poor fellows live where they do. I imagine when it gets rough it will be terrible down there. It is very close and stuffy as it is and there is not room for them all on deck at once so they have to take turns coming up for air. It takes so long to feed the poor old privates that they can only get in two meals a day. It seems to agree with them however as I can hear them singing out on the front deck.

Some of the officers thought we would pull out of harbor during Tuesday night but I heard some of the sailors say that we were not to leave until Wednesday afternoon. The beds were very comfortable and the fan kept up its good work so we had a good sleep and woke up to find New York still there and the same old rattle of the donkey engines loading our luggage. There were no more troops coming aboard now, only casual officers who had been excused to go to the Quartermaster to buy supplies. Finally about 2 PM tugs pulled away the barges at our sides, they took in all but one gang plank, and the front deck derricks were lashed down.

At 3:15 PM we were told that we would have to stay inside and be content to look out of the windows so that no one could see what kind of troops we were. At exactly four o'clock, May 22, 1918, the *Leviathan* started to move out. I cannot quite express the feeling that came over me as I saw the post I was squinting on slowly cover up the Lackawanna Tower. It was a combination of joy at going when I had so long wanted to go, and sorrow at leaving what I might never see again. I did not fear the submarines. I figure that I will get out all right if we do get struck. But I could not help thinking that my chances of seeing New York and home and the family that I left there were pretty small.

Slowly we pulled out and turned around. As we nosed down the harbor the boats on all sides tooted their whistles, the people in the office buildings waved from the windows, and those on the docks shouted and waved. It was an inspiring send-off, though we could not get the full benefit of it cooped up as we were inside. When we reached Battery Park we were allowed on deck again and we could get a last look at the Woolworth Building and the skyline of New York. As we passed Governor's Island I went to the other side of the boat to see the Statue of Liberty. It made a deep impression on me as I looked out between the lifeboats at that mighty emblem.

At 6:40 we slowed up and stopped to let our harbor pilot out. We had passed our last buoy marking our course and from there on we were free. Occasionally we could see a little sub chaser run along at a distance but as it was a little hazy we could not see much. At eight o'clock we were ordered inside and all lights were turned down. All windows were painted over and no smoking was allowed from the inside of D deck. They took up all our matches, cigar lighters, and flashlights. From then on till we reach the other side we are required to have our life belts with us. We even wear them to meals. I came down in my stateroom with my two bunkies, H. L. Land*, ASSRC, and B. F. Griffin, ASSRC. They are both aviators from Camp Dick. Nimocks also dropped in on us and the three played cards for a while.

Although last night was one of the most dangerous parts of our trip I slept finely until 7:30 this morning. The old boat was just as steady as if she were anchored, not even a vibration from the engines. You could not tell she was moving at all. This morning, May 23, it is very beautiful on deck. There is a crisp wind that is blowing with us and the sun shines on the whitecaps with a wonderful brightness. Everybody seems to be feeling finely and quite relieved. The nurses are all on deck talking of everything imaginable. I think the sailors have been trying to scare them. We ran into a school of fish which entertained us for some time by jumping out of the water. Well, I guess I will go up on deck as I have just about got this up to date.

Letter, On shipboard, no date permitted. Dear Family: About all I can say about this trip is that it has been perfectly wonderful. The weather has been glorious and the sea as calm as it ever can be. I am looking forward to my trip back already, when it comes. As one fellow said, "I could fight out this war on these lines if it took all Summer." However, as we near the scene of action I must confess that the old desire to get into it comes back. I have not the slightest idea what we are to do, nor where we are to be sent, but if I did I could not tell you anything about it as it would be censored. I will try to see Alice as soon as possible in order to deliver her goods and see her in her element. I don't know how long it will be before I get a chance to write you again, so remember no news is good news and if some of my letters go astray don't worry. Your loving son, Percival

Tuesday, May 28: It has been some time since I wrote in this last but I have been having too good a time. The life on this boat has certainly been great. Being a Second Lieutenant I have been put on the second mess so I don't have to get up until 7:30 at which time I am always awaked by "Hurry up there! Step along! Double line up ahead! Don't make so much noise! Double time!" etc. All of which commands are almost drowned out by the clatter and banging of mess kits and the stamping of numerous heavy hobnailed shoes in a mad desire to get food. The whole performance is quickened by a hunger that only comes to those who get but two meals a day.

After considerable discussion with my two bunkies as to the correct time we slowly came to the conclusion that if we want anything to eat we will have to hustle. Breakfast is a pretty good meal but it is generally a little bit cool. However the food is very good. At least that that the officers get. The enlisted men don't get much I am afraid. At least they seem mighty anxious to get what they do. After breakfast we generally go out on the front deck and watch for submarines, fish, and other ships. We have seen a bunch of ships. About four or five a day so far.

I generally see Bernadine Fennelly, a Red Cross nurse, who has been mighty good company on this trip. We have a mighty good time. She is a girl about 23 who has been through her three years' training and is in the 13th Base Hospital unit. She is from Superior, Wisconsin. Dinner comes at one o'clock and then the dancing begins. We have three bands on board and one plays after the other. Dancing all the afternoon and out on deck between. Time goes pretty fast and the finest weather possible. Only the slightest roll at times. At evening they have supper for us Second Lieutenants at 7:00 and the dancing keeps up right through. We generally dance until eight when the lights go out and they run us off the deck. There is only one thing to do and that is to go to the stateroom and write up this diary and letters, read, and play cards. Tonight we have been having a very lively discussion which I hope to be able to call off by 12:00. The secret has come out that the *Glendavid* has been sunk somewhere. We have no authority for it and it probably is a rumor. I am sure that if this old ship got hit there would be a bunch on this boat that would have a time getting off.

Saturday, June 8: It has been a long time since I wrote in this diary last as I had to pack it in my trunk. I will have better sense than to do that again. We have had a very interesting time since I packed up on the *Leviathan* the day before we came into Brest. The 30th of May, Decoration Day, will always be one to remember. The little convoy of five destroyers had been with us the entire day before, playing around this way and that like so many dogs out for a walk with their masters. All day long they shot out this way and that, zigzagging back and forth and continually signalling back to the *Leviathan*. That night we were ordered to sleep with our clothes on and the crew was to stay in their lifeboats. We were in the most dangerous part of the danger zone yet I cannot remember having a better sleep on the trip than I had that night.

We were told that we would be in sight of land by six o'clock the next morning so Bernadine and I agreed to get up early and watch for it. I got out on deck about ten minutes of six but no land was in sight. Only the same little group of six dogs [escort ships] dodging in and out around us. It was a wonderful day with hardly enough wind to stir up a ripple on the water. Bernadine showed up at about six thirty very much disappointed not to find a beautiful shore line with white houses silhouetted against a green background. However, we managed to kill the time until breakfast talking with an officer of the ship who said that we would not see land until at least eleven as we had gone out to sea during the night to avoid some submarines that were reported ahead of us.

At about 11:50 the entire deck was covered with people watching for the land when a sudden commotion started on the port side of the ship. I ran over to see what was the matter but before I could, there was a boom of a heavy gun and the whole ship shook with the shock. Our six inch rear gun had fired at something. I climbed up on a bunk and stuck my head out of the upper part of one of the windows just in time to hear another boom and see a cloud of yellow smoke come from the rear gun again. I looked out in the water to the rear and side of us. Crash!—there was a column of water went up about thirty feet mingled with black smoke. About a yard beyond where the shell had struck there was a little dark speck and a white streak of foam.

The speck disappeared but the white streak (the wake of the submarine) continued out away from us. Another boom and a splash and the streak disappeared. While this was going on the destroyers had kept their respective positions except that the one to our port rear had dropped back a little to get out of the way of our fire. They did not shoot as we had the heavier guns. Everything outside quieted down, the water where the shells had hit was white with bubbles, but as it was some distance away we could not see it very clearly. The destroyer to our rear steamed up to the spot [and] prepared to drop a depth charge but there was no use—the sub was either destroyed or had sunk too deep to be seen.

We had not gone five minutes when the back destroyer flashed up a signal and shot past us at about forty miles an hour letting out a dense smoke screen. Almost at the same instant the destroyer to our left at the side turned sharply around and started back. There was another white streak and a black speck coming in about the same place the other was only this time it was coming around towards us. In a minute more the sub would be in a position to fire, and there was a second's pause of dead silence. Every one of the two or three thousand pairs of eyes on that side of the boat was watching for a thin stream of bubbles to start towards us. Crash! Crash! The destroyer opened up with a full broad side, boom!

Three of our rear guns opened up at almost the same second. There was only a great cloud of spray where once there had been a periscope. Boom! Boom! the rear guns opened up again. Every shot fell right smack on the white blotch of water. The people on the boat just went wild. They lost all sense of fear and cheered like mad at the wonderful work of the gunners.

The destroyers signaled something and our guns stopped firing while the little hound of the sea shot over the place where the sub had been. There was evidently not enough left to make it worth while to drop a depth bomb. Once more we sailed calmly on at a great rate of speed. The harbor of Brest was right at hand and the pilot had come out in a little motor boat to guide us in, but there was no stopping for him. The subs had picked a good place but luckily they had given away their presence a little too soon. Had they waited a little longer they could have attacked us while we were standing still taking on the pilot. That was a close shave but we seemed to have escaped.

The people were noticing the beautiful harbor and the wonderful fortifications all around when someone yelled "Another submarine!" I looked where the others had appeared instinctively and there was another white streak just like the first two. We had slowed up a little on account of the shallow water but as the guns blazed out on that little white line, our ship seemed to jump ahead. One of the destroyers steamed up about a thousand yards ahead of us to show the channel and we went into the harbor at the rate of 32 miles an hour with the guns booming out behind. The sub was so far in the rear that there was not much danger so we stopped shooting and left it to the destroyers. By that time we were clear inside the harbor and there was not a chance for anything to get to us. The Huns had missed the chance of a lifetime and we had one in not [having] two subs to our credit. We turned off the power about a mile from our buoy and tried to stop for it, [but] even by reversing we went quite a ways beyond our mark.

The harbor at Brest is very beautiful. The shore at its outside comes up to steep bluffs on each side of the narrow entrance and gradually levels off again. It is like a great gateway with massive pillars on each side. The whole top of the bluff is covered with forts which would make the harbor impossible to take I imagine. Inside the harbor there is another bluff running out into the bay, where there is another large fort. There were a great many ships at anchor, mostly freighters. It seemed that they have only a few docks and therefore are not able to handle shipping very well. We had to unload into lighters.

The nurses and most of the troops were taken off the ship the same afternoon but we (the casual officers) were kept on until the first of June, just 48 hours after we landed. During that time the jackers worked day and night coaling up while one battalion of troops unloaded the ship. Nimocks and I spent most of our time looking over the great old boat to see really what she was like. We went over her from stem to stern and even climbed up the rear mast. Time certainly did hang heavy for those two days but finally we got off.

We were ordered to Porte Maison Barracks but on arrival there we found that they had no accommodations for us so all the casuals took out quarters at the Hotel Moderne which was run by the YMCA. My first night there was a disastrous one. The bed bugs in my sector made an unexpected attack and took three beds including mine. They came over the top in mass formation and took a large section at the point of the bayonet. I got a new room in the morning. That evening I spent locating my baggage and seeing an operetta with Nimocks. We could not understand a word but the singing was pretty good. I met a very interesting French officer there whom we saw later in town. His name was Lieutenant Serrant [of the] 72nd Regiment.

Sunday morning [2 June] I went up to the barracks to look up Bernadine. I found her without much difficulty and we went over to see a chateau nearby where a Countess Somebody lived. The Countess was not at home so the gate was locked. We walked around a while and then climbed over the back wall. After seeing the whole place around the sides we went up to the house. It was a very old place with a chapel built on to the side of it. The whole thing was covered with climbing roses which were in full bloom. It was a beautiful place. After jumping over the wall again (about an 8 foot wall) we went back to the barracks for dinner. That afternoon

Bernadine and I walked to town and went through a very old chateau which was right on the sea front of Brest. The foundations of the old place were laid by the Romans in 100 BC and the building was finished in the 14th century. We went through the dungeons and prisons and torture chambers which were way underground. It was very interesting.

We went up to the Moderne for dinner and met Nimocks there. After a good American meal we went down to the pier and hired a little sail boat for an hour and a man to run it. We went out into the harbor and found that it was considerably rougher than it looked from the shore. However we did not mind the salt spray much and had lots of fun dodging in among the ships of the port. As there were no trucks running when we got back to town we had to walk out to camp, about three miles, and take Bernadine home. The next day (Monday) Nimocks and I did not get up till noon and then we shopped most of the time. Brest is not much of a place. There are about 90,000 people there but it is very dirty and had no water system or drainage system before the Americans took it over for a troop port. The people are very poor and the town looks as if it had been absolutely drained by the war. These poor old French people are all worn out, but they still have an incorrigible spirit. They will never quit until they have put in their last ounce. They certainly are glad to see the Americans come.

Tuesday Nimocks and I went out to Porte Maison at twelve o'clock and met Julia and Bernadine. After the girls had raided the kitchen and got some white bread and butter we started off on a picnic. Although we did not have much to eat, still the sardines, olives, chocolates, cheese, and strawberries were pretty good. After the meal we took some pictures and went over to see an old church at Lambezelath. It was a mighty interesting old place built in about 1600. We got a beautiful view of the country around from the steeple.

On our way back to the barracks we passed a high wall evidently enclosing a country place. We rang the doorbell and after struggling through considerable French we got in to see the gardens and the house. The old lady who met us inside took great pleasure in showing us her gardens which were very beautiful. Her grandson could speak a little English so we got along finely. When I asked for some water they insisted that we go in and have some white wine which the old lady insisted was older than she was and wonderfully good. The others took some but Bernadine and I stood out against it and insisted on water. The whole visit was very interesting and we had a peach of a time.

Wednesday we got our orders to go to Blois on the following day [Fig. 5]. We brought the girls in to dinner but we did not do much except look around the town. When we got back to camp we found that the nurses had got their orders to go the next morning. So we promised to see them off. Thursday was a busy day. We got up early and went down to fix up our baggage and see off the nurses. I was mighty sorry to see them go as I had had a mighty good time with them all. Bernadine gave me a little luck model of Saint Joseph which is guaranteed to bring good luck at all times. I prize it quite highly as she had carried it around with her for about ten years.

That afternoon we all took the train at 2:55 for Blois. After a very beautiful trip we arrived at Le Mans at 12:30 and had to stop for the night and take our train for Tours at 8:30 the next morning. That was some night. We went all over the town of Le Mans but no hotel would take us in. At about 2 [AM] I had one last bright hunch and got out my bedding roll from the baggage room, set up my cot on the platform, and went to sleep. It got pretty cold and the trains passed through pretty often so we did not sleep too much. At five o'clock Clark* and I went up to town to see the place. We found two very old and beautiful cathedrals, one built in the 11th century—Notre Dame de la Couteau—and the other built in the 12th century—St. Julian. The country is having continuous mass or something similar at present to try to stop the German drive on Paris. People were entering and leaving the churches all day and all night. These Catholics have certainly very great faith.

The trip from Le Mans to Tours was lost on me as I slept all the way. At Tours we found that our train for Blois was to leave at 1:05. That was too early to suit us so we decided to stay over until the next day. It was then about 12:00 so I got dinner and then hiked for the Aviation Field. I found Alice standing in front of her

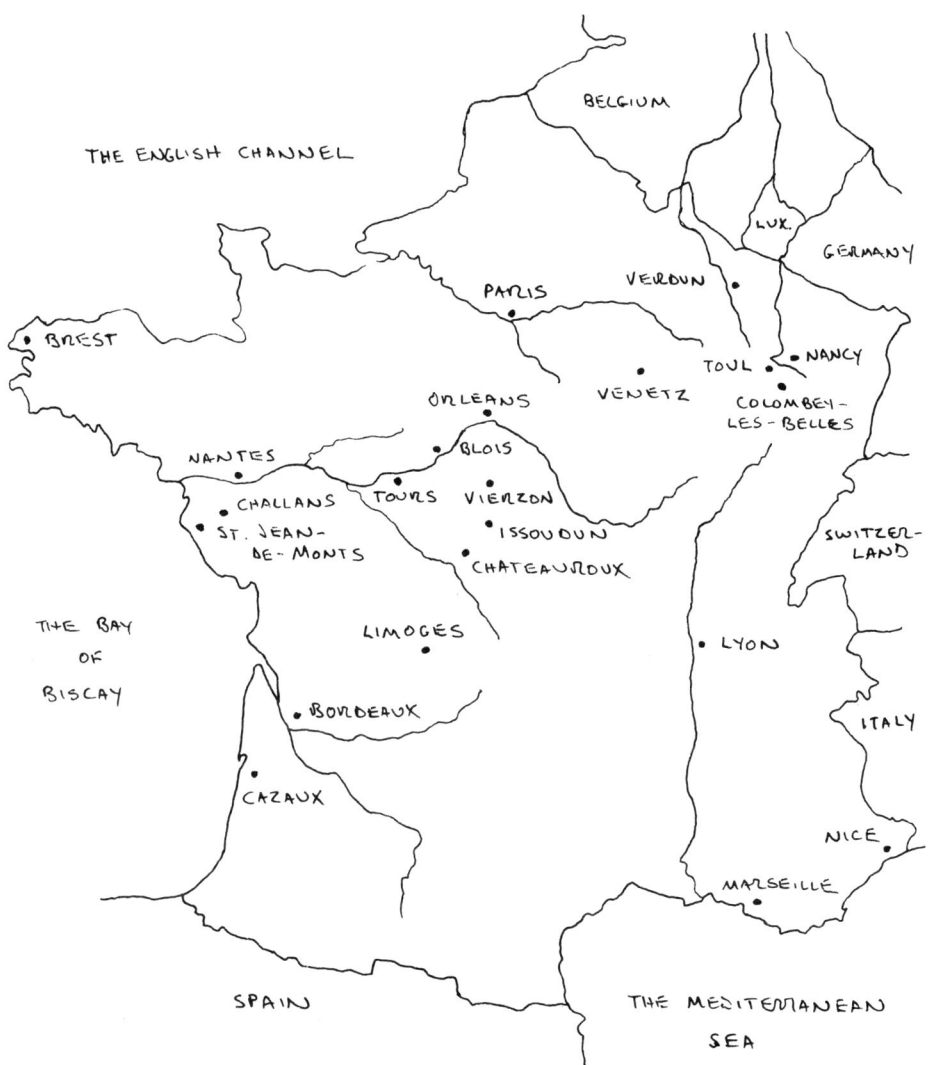

Fig. 5. Map of France

canteen talking with Sam Slaughter*. A scene followed which had been my dream for a good many months. Sam got Russ in a short time and we had a great reunion. When Russ went to a class Alice and I took a walk over the camp and saw everything. The Field is primarily for training beginners though they do teach some observers. After his class Russ joined us and we had a great old talk in Al's room all about everything. Russ showed me his diary and scrapbook which are both great. After dinner Russ and I went out on the field for a while to watch the flying. The Caudrons they use are fine training planes. I spent the night with some of Al's officer friends. I believe the dear old girl knows everybody in that school. The fellows are certainly all crazy about her and cannot say enough of the good she does them by her smiling "Good morning!" or "Hello!"

I left this morning on the 8:52 train after a very nice ride to the train in a motorcycle. I sent a cablegram home. We arrived here at Blois about eleven o'clock and got signed in and fixed up by dinner. This is a distributing center for casual officers so we will just have to wait till we get our orders. We have very good quarters, practically no duties, and fine food. I spend most of my time writing up this thing and writing letters. I met Stella MacNaughton this evening. She has not been well and is staying here as this is the best place for food in France.

Sunday, June 9: It was a mighty pretty day today and nothing much to do. I spent most of the morning between roll calls writing letters. As Clark was on duty I did not go to the chateau but went for a walk instead. After buying a little map of Blois and vicinity I started out across the bridge and had a peach of a walk up through the Foret de Russe south of Blois. It was beautiful walking and the only cool place around. Coming back the road ran right along the bank of the Loire for about a mile. Nimocks and I went downtown in the evening to get some water as the supply was off from noon on out here at camp. Later in the evening I made out some copies of my travel orders and went to bed.

Monday, June 10: Cold rainy day today without much outlook at first. We had a lecture on gas attacks this morning and had to go through tear gas. The lecture was very interesting as the fellow that gave it knew his subject well. I hope I never get in a very heavy attack. The exposure to tear gas was not much as the masks worked very well. When we took them off though it certainly made the tears come.

Tuesday, June 11: Today the Captain got the bright idea that the Aviators needed drilling. As a result we got it for two and a half hours this morning. After which I spent the rest of the morning packing up Alice's things and putting in a mileage voucher. In the afternoon we were ordered to take the gas drill again. For some reason or another I could not find the company at the proper time so I did not go. After sleeping and loafing around for some time I tried to get permission to go to Tours. All I could get out of anybody was that it was impossible. Finally I saw Major Glendinning*. He told me that our orders would be out very soon for Tours and Issodun and he would try to get me on the list for the former. The good news of orders did me pretty well and I got treated to all the chocolate and sandwiches I could eat down town. I ended up with a good hot bath and went out to camp for bed.

Wednesday, June 12: The orders did not come out this morning so we were ordered on another drill. However, this time we went on a hike. After a walk of about three miles we stopped on the banks of the Loire and all went in for a swim. The water came straight from Greenland but it felt pretty good on a hot day. This afternoon Nimocks and I went out to the Chambord Chateau on hired wheels. It was about 18 kilometers but we stopped at a little inn on the way and got refreshments in the way of omelets, bread, French fried potatoes, and strawberries. The Chateau was very beautiful. It was built in 1550 and it is supposed to be the finest in the country. We tried to get a few supplies in town after we got back and among other things we ordered cookies. I don't know what they were made of, but it only took one to make me sick. I think I will keep away from them hereafter.

Saturday, June 15: The last two days have been uneventful. We have just been waiting around for orders and not doing much but sticking around. Today an order came out but as I was not on it I gave up hope and hired a bicycle for a day. I started at 3:15 for Tours or as near as I could get there. The road was right down the bank of the Loire through very beautiful country. About 12 kilometers down I passed the Chateau of Chaumont which was across the river on a kind of bluff set in among the trees. It certainly was a beautiful place. I went on down the river until I came to a bridge across it leading over to another town and a large chateau which was evidently a hospital for wounded. I crossed over and went up to see the chateau which turned out to be the Chateau of Ambois. A lady took me through it but as she could not speak a word of English I did not get much out of what she said. However, the building and the garden were very beautiful. This was more of a castle than most of the others as it was fortified with turrets on all sides with places to drop down bombs, stones, and hot lead.

After seeing the castle I went back to the town and got a fine meal at the Lion d'Or Hotel. On the way [back] I took the road on the opposite side of the river from the way I came down. All the roads in France seem to be wonderful. Perhaps it is because there is so much touring through this country during peace time.

Sunday, June 16: I started out this morning at about 8:30 after I was sure that there would be no orders and got my bicycle. Although I was considerably sore from the day before, still I started out for Orleans about 65 kilometers away. The road lay right up the river and it was as beautiful as the one going downstream to Tours. The road itself was very dusty and rough. All the worse on my more sensitive parts. About twenty fellows went by me going the same way at a great speed. They were also on bicycles but they were having some kind of a race. They were trying to cover the 280 kilometers to Paris in nine hours. I guess they made it all right if they kept up the speed at which they were going. I met a Morroccan who rode several miles with me. Finally he dropped off quite sore because I would not stop for a drink with him.

I arrived at Orleans about 12:30 and went right up to the Hotel Moderne. There I washed up and took dinner. The people sitting near me seemed quite surprised when I insisted on water and I guess they thought I could not afford anything else, because at the end of the meal two French privates who were sitting across the way held a consultation and ordered the best champagne they could afford. Much to my surprise they poured out three glasses and very proudly handed one glass to me. Gee whiz, I did feel cheap and at the same time highly embarrassed as I could not speak French well enough to tell them in the most polite way that I never drank anything but water. I just did the best I could but I could see that my explanation was not very satisfactory. I will have to either learn French or take to drink. I will try the former.

Just as I was leaving the table an American officer sat down. He asked me where I was from. I told him and he said that he was going back to Blois that evening in his car and would take me with him. After I accepted his invitation I discovered that it was against the law for me to be in that town and that my friend was the Intelligence Officer of Blois. It was part of his job to arrest me and turn me over to the Provost Marshal. I saw the joke on me and I made such good use of the old excuse of ignorance that he let me off (from arrest but not from going home with him). I spent the afternoon riding all over the town and vicinity. It is a typical French town with a large square in the center and roads branching out in all directions like the spokes of a wheel. There is a large statue of Jeanne d'Arc mounted on horseback in the center of the square. I met my friend at six thirty and had a fine ride home. After supper I found that orders were coming out the next day so I packed up.

PART 3

Flying Training, 3rd Aviation Instruction Center, Issoudun, France, 17 June to 6 August 1918

[Gates was stationed at Issoudun from June 18th through August 5th. When he arrived at Issoudun, Gates found an active and well-organized training center. After a discouraging start during the fall and winter of 1917–18, when the first students had to help prepare the field and its facilities, a productive routine had been established by the spring of 1918, and students assigned to Issoudun were making progress through the training program according to the intended plan. The Issoudun training center, located about twenty miles north of Chateauroux and one hundred and thirty miles south of Paris, consisted initially of nine separate flying fields used by students in the advanced flying training program. Three other fields were used by students in bombing and observation training. Those pilots who desired to become pursuit pilots (pilotes de chasse), as opposed to bomber or observation pilots, worked hard to follow a specific progression through the nine training fields.

Gates' first stop was Field 1, part of the Main Field, where he reviewed high speed taxi procedures in "Rouleurs," Moraine monoplanes with 50 horsepower Gnome rotary engines. These single-seat aircraft did not possess adequate power to become fully airborne, but were intended to help students learn ground-handling techniques, particularly in coordinating the use of the rudder during takeoff and landing. He then moved to nearby Field 2 for some dual instruction in the Nieuport Model 81, powered by an 80 horsepower Le Rhone rotary engine. This aircraft was also known as a 23 Meter Nieuport because its total wing surface was 23 square meters. After demonstrating proficiency in engine operation and landing techniques, Gates was cleared to Field 3 on the 7th of July.

At Field 3, also a part of the Main Field complex, Gates flew a solo (single-seat) version of the Nieuport Model 81. After demonstrating proficiency in takeoffs and landings, he proceeded to Field 9, where he flew 18 Meter Nieuports (Model 83), powered by 80 horsepower Le Rhone rotary engines. Mastery of the single-seat Model 83 at Field 9 was crucial, for those pilots who displayed hesitancy or difficulty in flying the Model 83 were diverted out of the chasse program and were directed into bomber or reconnaissance training programs. Gates surmounted this hurdle successfully, and completed his required flying at Fields 3 and 9 in only five days.

Lieutenant Gates then reported to Field 5, where he flew the 15 Meter Nieuport Model 24, powered by an 80 horsepower Le Rhone engine. At Field 5 he practiced airwork and aerobatics, developing proficiency in maneuvers he had not previously flown. Field 5 was located at some distance from the Main Field complex, and the training complex included a separate barracks and dining facility. Six days later, on the 17th of July, he completed all required training at Field 5 and moved to nearby Field 7, where he flew cross-country and formation flights in the 120 horsepower Le Rhone-powered 15 Meter Nieuport. A week later he moved to his final training field, Field 8, where he practiced gunnery and simulated air combat.

Gates concluded his stay at Issoudun with two familiarization flights in aircraft he had not previously flown—a Moraine monoplane and a Sopwith Camel. After receiving a farewell briefing from the school commander, Lt. Carl Spaatz (the "Tooey" Spaatz of

Flying Training

WWII fame), Gates departed Issoudun for aerial gunnery school at St. Jean-de-Monts. He had flown during 27 of the 49 days of his Issoudun training program, adding 60 hours to his total flying time, which amounted to almost 93 hours.

Flight training at Issoudun was no less hazardous than it had been at Park Field; Gates' diary entries record the deaths of at least fifteen students. On the 24th of June he notes that "three weeks ago they killed about a man a day for over a week." On the 16th of July he comments that there are now 44 graves in the Issoudun graveyard. Gates himself narrowly avoided an accident on the 12th of July when he turned abruptly into his wingman's line of flight; on the 2nd of August he was involved in a midair collision with another pilot. However, he completed the program successfully, earning the coveted assignment as a "pilote de chasse."]

Monday, June 17: I got my orders at last to Issoudun. They told me at the station that I could not go through Tours as that town was closed, so I sent off all my baggage to Issoudun and took the next train for Tours. When I was about two kilos out of Tours I tried to get off the train so as to escape the Military Police at the station but no such luck. I hadn't gone ten steps before an MP called out "Where are you going, Lieutenant?" I said I was going out to the road. He only smiled and said, "Sorry, sir, but you will have to get back on the train; too many officers have tried that before."

At Tours I went out toward the telegraph office so as to get out the side gate of the station. I was just about there when a guard stepped out with a broad grin and said that he was there to keep officers from going out any way except through the regular Provost Marshal's office. At the Provost Marshal's office I lined up behind about ten other officers who were all ordered to Tours. I walked in behind them and put down my orders just as if they were to Tours instead of Issoudun. The Marshal never looked at them but just stamped them "Passed" and let me go.

I saw Alice and Russell for about three hours and delivered all the goods I brought over to them. They are in fine spirits though Alice worries too much about Russ and me. I got a ride into town about 10 o'clock but could not find a place to sleep. Finally I hid in a dark room in the YMCA Hotel and lay down on a little couch about four feet long. I did not sleep much but it was better than nothing.

Tuesday, June 18:   I went down to the station early and got a bite to eat. There I met twenty-five of the 13th Base Hospital unit nurses who came over on the boat. Bernadine Fennelly was not with them as she had gone to Paris with another detachment. I got to Issoudun at 12:20 and came out to camp on a truck and touring car. I finished reporting all right but I could not get my blanket roll. So I had to go to bed without bedding after writing some letters and hearing a very good concert by the St. Louis Quartet.

Letter, June 18, Issoudun.   Dear Grace: I am [now] at the 3rd Aviation Instruction Center, Issoudun. I stopped in to see Alice and Russell on my way here yesterday and found them in wonderful spirits. Alice is certainly making good. She knows everybody in the camp and she has a smile and a word of greeting for each one. I never knew she had so much spirit, pep, and quick wit in her. Everybody is just crazy to do anything possible for her. When I went to see her and Russell this last time I delivered all the clothes I brought over for them. Russ is doing very well in his flying and has the same idea I have, namely, that there is no hurry, and the thing to do is play safe all the time and get all the training possible. You need not worry about me as I have at least a month of ground school work before I do any flying. But when I do start, believe me I am going to take it easy and slow.

I will be here a *long* time. Russell will probably be down here in a month or so and then we can go on together. This is a great place. I wish I could describe it to you but I will wait till I find out what one is permitted to write. Don't worry and think on a rainy day, "Where is my wandering boy tonight?" for like as not he is having a great old time, in the canteen, or seeing some chateaux or ruins or something. I don't want to make you all jealous, but if you want to have a good time, you'd better come over here. We will have a great time over here after the war, believe me.

I am getting along finely with my French, and I know all the country around where I have been. The roads here are very solid and they certainly are fine. None in the United States could stand what these do. It is lots of sport to talk with the country people. They love to talk with Americans and if you give a man a cigarette he will do anything for you. I carry cigarettes to give to the poor fellows though I have not started to smoke myself. I promise that I will not start either unless it is necessary for some good reason. I've not touched a drop of anything except water, milk, cocoa, and coffee either. That is going some as the water is very bad in some places, and I have had to go without anything for some time. I must stop for tonight.

The next day: It has rained off and on all day today, so I have not had much pep to do anything. We had a couple of classes which are the start of a regular course. We are living in very good barracks and fairly comfortable beds. Mine will be more comfortable when my bedding roll comes this evening and I get some blankets to keep me warm. There was a slip somewhere last night and I slept light. The food is rather plain, but good and plenty of it. Also there is a good YMCA canteen here which sells the same things that Alice does. Every once in a while I run across a fellow or two who has been at Alice's school and they cannot say enough about her work there, and how much it has meant to them to know her there. I will have a hard time living up to the reputation Alice and Russell have made for the Gates family. Send all of us all the pictures you can; you don't know what they mean to us. Well, I must stop and go to dinner. Most lovingly, Percival

Letter, June 20. Dear Russ: I have been over here a couple of days now as you know but I have not seen enough of it to know how I'm going to like it. The men over here are the most discouraged and pepless lot I have met yet. I hope I don't catch the fever. I think the worst spell is over now and business will pick up right along. The ground course is not quite as long as I thought it would be.

So far it is quite interesting and very easy. There is lots of good dope in it though. I am getting stronger and stronger for the idea of taking one's time and playing safe. This is no playground as it is in the states. Tell Alice she must not worry about me, and that you will be here before I start flying. You know as much about this place as I do so there is no use in my trying to describe it as it would only be censored. I have not received any mail yet though I expect it every day. I wrote to Headquarters to forward any that was there so I will have some soon. Well there isn't much news. Just take good care of yourself and Alice. Your loving brother, Percival

Monday, June 24:   I have been here almost a week now and I think I can write a more correct account of this place than if I had tried when I first came. Our duties are very simple and easy. We have from three to six classes a day in ground school work such as engines, bombing, machine guns (Vickers), trap shooting, machine gun shooting, pistol shooting, courts-martial, etc. The classes are very easy and if they don't give us too much they will be quite interesting. We have this work to fill our time until we can get on the flying list.

The morale around here is about as low as any place I ever saw. These poor fellows have been in France so long, doing nothing, that their spirit is broken. Then about three weeks ago they killed a man a day for over a week. That broke the back of the school and they are just recovering. The Sunday before I got here a nurse was killed in an airplane accident. Yesterday and the day before two more men were killed. However, I think that most of the trouble is mental and in some cases due to feeling poorly when flying. For the reason that we were told all kinds of wild stories when we got here, I have not tried to write up this diary until I got the facts.

This is a very finely equipped school [Fig. 6]. Everything that is necessary or even desirable for a good thorough training is here. The planes are almost all Nieuports with a few others mixed in. The course is about as follows: first, some ground school work, then a little training on Rouleurs, then some dual control on Nieuport 23s followed by solo work on the same. Then after you

Flying Training

Fig. 6. Flying Field at Issoudun, France (OHTM)

have done some work on 18s you either go on to 15s or bombing training (cross country and formations). I hope to take the 15s and go on to *chasse* though I will probably change my mind later.

We have pretty good barracks with double decked bunks. I was lucky enough to get a lower. Saturday McCoy and I went for a walk out in the country through Paudy. From the top of a tower which we were inspecting, we saw a chateau out in the woods. It looked pretty good so we made for it. We walked right in the front gate and up to the house just as if we had been invited. After wandering around a bit we got up nerve enough to ask for a drink. That broke the ice and we were invited to sit down. There was a very nice young lady there and her mother. Neither was very good looking but we had lots of fun trying to talk French. Finally we had tea. No sugar but honey instead. After tea they took us to see their tennis court and made us promise to come over again and play. We had a good time and have got a place to go for a good walk. I went down to Issoudun Sunday but there was nothing there. I left some pictures to be developed.

Letter, 24 June. Dear Family: I am still at Issoudun and I will be here for some time yet. So far I have had no flying. Only ground school work the same as we had in the states, except that this work is adapted to the conditions that we will actually have later on. I cannot think of a course I had at Georgia Tech that is of any value to me now. Therefore this ground work is quite interesting and very desirable. Also this school is very beautifully equipped in every way. I don't know when I will start flying but when I do you can be assured that I am getting as good training as can be gotten.

I have met several fellows here who have been at the school with Alice and almost every one has said, "Well you don't know what your sister has done for us fellows, or how much her smile has meant." The fellows who spent the winter over here had a mighty hard time of it and I know there were a lot of fellows who will never forget "that smile of Miss Gates." You would hardly know her here in action, with a smile and a cheery word for everyone. Not that she has not always had that disposition, but she has not had so much of an opportunity to use it. For instance, as she walked over the camp with me she would stop at a sign "Keep Out" and say, "I never can see a sign like that that I don't walk in and see why I should keep out," much to the delight of the men behind the sign. We stopped at one window and she introduced me to Steve who cordially invited us in. "Steve," she said, "you've invited me to come in and sit down at least ten times, though I looked your office over from end to end and there isn't a thing to sit on but the floor." She has a good time just giving others a smile and a word.

We have a canteen here that helps out a lot. It is always a fine place to write. There is generally some kind of an entertainment in the evening. And there is always something to eat if you don't get enough supper. I am very strong for the YMCA and the work it is doing over here, not so much for the religious, though they have very good services, but for the work they do in making life easier and more comfortable for us all. The Red Cross does very good work at the stations along the railroad lines, just the same as in the states, but it does not do so much in the camps. Well as I have told all the interesting and uninteresting news and have exhausted most of the topics of the present day I will close. Lovingly, Percival

Friday, June 28: The work has been pretty steady this week so far. We get about six classes a day, mostly machine gun. However once in a while we get some types of machines, bombing, engine test, and Nieuport flying mixed in. Wednesday I found Louis Soule and he took me for a ride in a 23 dual control [Nieuport aircraft]. When we got in the air he signaled for me to take the controls. I did and found that she was just about like a Curtiss in the air except that she was a lot more sensitive and faster. The first thing I knew Louis was talking in my ear. I looked back to see where he was and found that he had climbed out of his seat and was sitting astride the fuselage between the front and rear seats. He must have had a lot of faith in the machine to take a chance like that with me running it. When he had got back in, he took control and put her in a very steep sideslip. Then he let go of all controls and let her take herself out, which she did very quickly. The same day (June 26) I got my first letters from home, two from Grace. Yesterday I got one from Lucia. There was a very good show in the Y last night. One fellow on the guitar was especially good. Our squadron, 111, has been put on Rouleurs. We went out this morning but there were too many others ahead of us so we are to report this afternoon.

Letter, June 28. Dear Mother: Everything is going finely here. Though they keep us pretty busy the work is quite interesting. It will be better still from now on as I am starting flying today. This is quite a little sooner than I expected you see. I am going to take it slowly and see if I cannot let Russ catch up with me. He is not here yet but he will be soon. Day before yesterday, I met Helen Harrison's fiance, Lt. Soule. He is a very fine flyer and is at present testing machines. He took me for a ride and let me run the machine a while to prove that it was really easier to control than a Curtiss. The landing will be the only hard part I believe. Tell Helen that Louis is looking finely and is doing wonderfully well.

We are having the most wonderful weather; long days, bright sunshine and only nice and warm, not hot as it is at home. This is a great climate all right for flying. I am keeping up my diary pretty well. There are some things that are quite interesting that I cannot write. Though we censor our own mail we cannot put in anything that a regular censor would not let through. You see the idea is not that we cannot tell our folks things, but that we cannot put anything in a letter that would interest the Kaiser were he to get hold of it. Therefore we write as though each letter was to be taken by some German spy. I would almost rather have someone else censor my mail. I am sure I could get away with more than I than I can with myself. Well I must stop and go over to dinner. I write pretty often, so if you don't hear you will know that my letters are being held up somewhere and will come through later. Your loving son, Percival

Sunday, June 30: I have been here [in France] just one month and I am still perfectly content to stick it out. Not that I don't have to anyhow, but I am having a pretty good time of it. Friday we did not go out on the Rouleurs as too many got busted up. However

Flying Training

our time came Saturday morning. It was fairly good but there was a little too much cross wind to be safe. They are the funniest things in the world to watch, especially when there is a little wind. A Rouleur is a "thing" (neither airplane nor automobile) which runs along the ground. It has wings but it cannot fly. It looks like an airplane, with fuselage, tail, elevators, etc. The idea is to get in and run on down the field at a pretty good clip and keep it straight. You run it a little bit faster each time till you get it up to top speed (about 50 mph). They go bouncing and flopping around like a chicken with its head off. There are two machines to a field and it is a circus to see them race along, slow up and spin around on one wheel, or tip over, catch a wing in the ground, and do a regular cart wheel.

One fellow broke an axle on a "cheval de bois" and threw his machine head over tea pot. The propellor went in a hundred pieces and the machine ended over on its back. I was the first one to arrive on the scene of the tragedy. There was the fellow curled up in a little ball with his head sticking through the top of the wing. I thought he must be pretty badly hurt as he had not tried to disentangle himself, but when I got a look at his face I found that he was laughing so hard he couldn't move.

Another fellow went tearing down the field about as fast as he could go. He was trying so hard to get his machine straight that he did not see that he was going right into the other machine. They hit at right angles with a great crash. I don't know what was the matter with the fellow but he did not seem to hear the crash, or see the splinters fly, or even know that half of his wing had been chewed off by the propellor of the other machine. He just kept right on going just as if nothing had happened [Fig. 7].

Sunday we were to get into flying but it did not work out. Another fellow had been killed the day before and it was too windy to fly. I started to walk down town but got picked up by a motorcycle about half way. The stores were most all closed though, so I could not get my pictures developed. I was lucky and got a ride home on a truck. It was a Fiat and could make about 40. We made it most of the way. I went to evening service at 8:00 and heard a good talk by Dr. Coffin of New York.

Fig. 7. Wrecked Rouleurs, Issoudun, France (OHTM)

Letter, June 30. Dear Auntie: I am enclosing a couple of pictures that were taken during my little visit with Alice and Russell. I am in perfect health, I never have felt better. You can also see that Russ and Alice are just great [Fig. 8]. It is almost impossible for me to visit Alice often but I may be able to work it again somehow. Fellows come from there all the time so I can keep pretty good track of what Russ is doing and how Alice is. I started my preliminary work yesterday, and today or tomorrow I will start to fly. I doubt if Russ will be over for about two weeks now as I just got word from a fellow from Tours that Russ had just soloed. He will have quite a little more work to do there before he comes over. Well I must stop now and write to Alice. Lovingly, Percival

Letter, June 30. Dear Alice: This is just a note enclosing the two pictures I took over there. Your friend Lt. Shadrack looked me up when he was over here. He also looked me up again before he went back. He's a mighty nice fellow. A fellow named Baker looked me up too. He was very kind and offered to help me out any time I got into trouble. So far I have kept pretty clear of it. Please tell that rascal Russ to hurry up and write. As I cannot hold up any longer I have to take things as they come and go ahead. Tell Russ to take all the work he can get there as it will help out greatly here. Slim chance of getting over to see you the 4th so don't wait for me. Your loving brother, Percival

Monday, July 1: My dates are pretty easy to remember as everything seems to happen on the last or the first day of the month. This morning we had a fine schedule, 8:00 traps [shooting], [and] I managed to get 11 out of 25. That is fairly good as we are using little "clean-up" guns with short barrels and a big scatter ineffective at over 40 yards. Then we had pistol shooting. That was good fun and fine practice. We use .45 automatics. The class in Military Law did not hatch so we had nothing until 11:00 when we got out for drill. After dinner we had nothing until 4:00. I wrote several letters.

The flying was called off on account of wind until later in the evening. At 8:00 we were called out. Woody and I had the luck to get on a new list so we were first up. I just had one ride of about

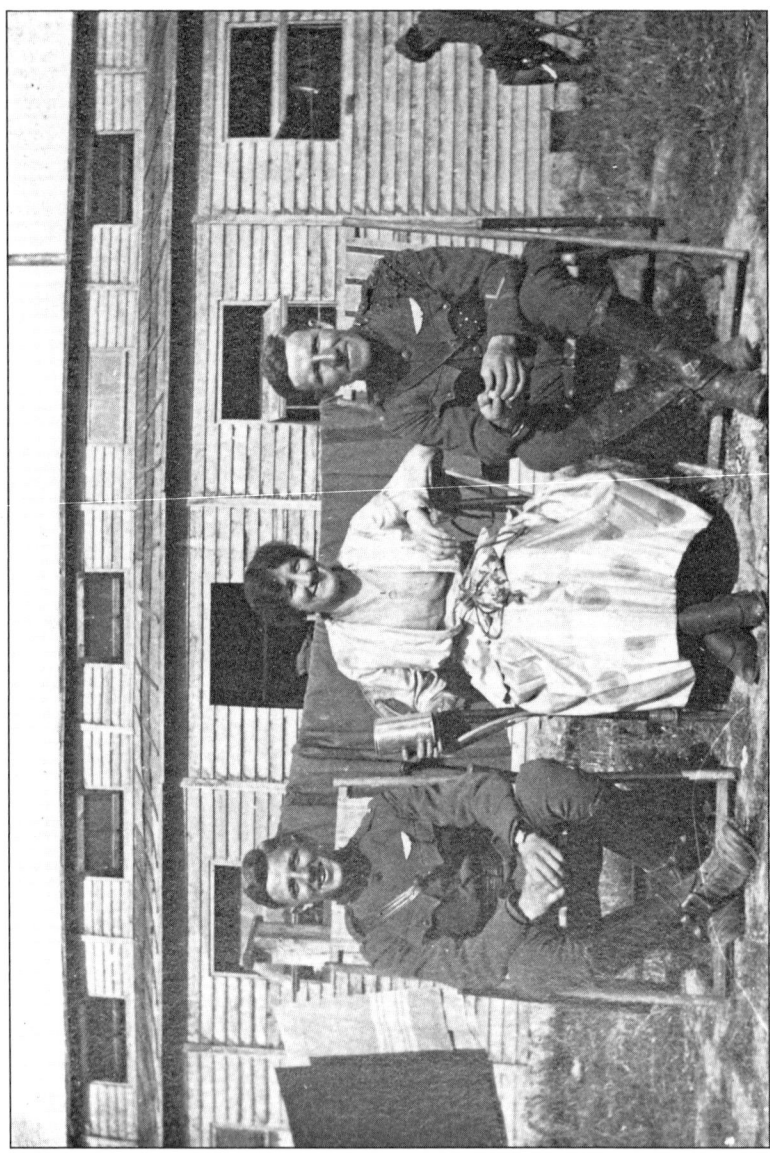

Fig. 8. Percival, Alice, and Russell Gates, Tours, France (OHTM)

15 minutes in which [the instructor] gave me the controls. It was a wonderful evening and the air was calm as glass. The fields were all marked off in little squares so that the country below looked like a checkerboard.

Ain't It Fine Today

What's the use of always weepin'
   Makin' trouble last?
What's the use of always keepin'
   Thinkin' of the past?
Each must have his tribulation
   Water with his wine.
Life it ain't no celebration.
   Trouble? I've had mine—
   But today is fine.

Sure this world is full of trouble
   I ain't said it ain't.
Lord! I've had enough an' double
   Reason for complaint.
Rain an' storm have come to fret me
   Skies were often grey.
Thorns and brambles have beset me
   On the road—but say
   Ain't it fine today!

It's today that I am livin'
   Not a month ago.
Havin', losin', talkin', givin',
   As time wills it so.
Yesterday a cloud of sorrow
   Fell across the way.
It may rain again tomorrow
   It may rain—but say
   Ain't it fine today.

Issoudun
July 1, 1918

Letter, July 2. Dear Alice: I have started flying and will finish 23 dual control tomorrow probably. 23 singles takes about one day, but we don't fly till next week as we have the 4th, 5th, and 6th off. I tried to get a pass to get over to see you, but could not do it. I think I will stay here. Please write some time. Tell Russ to take every minute he can as it will save time at this end. I must stop now as lights are out. Love, Percival

Thursday, July 4:   I was stopped short in writing up my last entry and I have not written since then. Tuesday we only had one class and drill in the morning. In the afternoon we had a full flying time. I got in 41 minutes and five landings. Then Lt. Welty, my instructor, insisted that I go over to the tester. I took a couple of rides in which I put the tester [check pilot] into a skid, sideslip, and made corrections for whatever he did to the machine. Everything went finely except the landings and takeoffs which were weak. He advised me to go back to Lt. Welty for more practice on those things as they would count against me on the next field. We got in about 9:30, pretty tired.

Wednesday the day went about the same. It was pretty rough for flying in the afternoon but I managed to get in eight minutes and three hops. We quit flying at 8:00 to go to the dance. I went to a show in the Y which was very good. After that I got all fired up and went to the Red Cross dance. It was too crowded to dance much but there were a lot of American girls there from various Canteens and they had some ice cream and cake which reminded me more of America than most anything else. I got to bed about 1:00 very sleepy. This morning I did not get up until nine o'clock. I went down to Issoudun to get some films I was having printed but they were not finished yet. I took dinner there and came home. I went to the track meet for a while with Woody and then went to sleep.

Letter, July 4.   Dear Family: This is the first letter of this month so I am going to give a summary of all the letters I have received from you. I will try to do it about once a month after this so that you can keep track of the letters you write me. It will work out very nicely if you will each keep a book with the dates of your letters in it. I number mine so you can tell from that how they are coming. I

Flying Training

have received one letter from Father dated June 8th. Two letters from Mother dated respectively May 26 and June 5th, the last one forwarded by Auntie. None of Auntie's have come through as yet. Three from Lucia dated May 26th, June 2, and June 9th. Three from Grace dated May 23rd, May 28th, and June 3rd. So you can see there is quite a little mail that has not come yet. I am expecting a big haul tomorrow, as we will get two days' mail in one. Well, that covers the mail subject for June pretty thoroughly I guess.

I have started flying and have had my first instruction on these planes. The first thing we had was a little work on Rouleurs. They are little machines with clipped wings that just tear all over the ground. The game is to run them keeping in as straight a line as possible and stop without making a "cheval de bois" which in French means merry-go-round. It is about as good sport as I have had yet. The little rascals go about 50 miles an hour, I think; at least it feels that way. They seemed to be possessed with the evil one, and I believe they are, for they shoot off this way and that, spin around on one wheel and seem to have a magnetic attraction for each other. They would be quite dangerous if they were not so light and did not have wings to tip over on and break the fall. As it is, they are just ludicrous playthings.

I managed to get through without busting anything so I have been put on flying with the rest of my section. The flying is a good deal easier than I expected. I have had about an hour and I expect to solo Sunday or Monday. One of our class has already been soloed. The landings are the only hard part and I am getting them down now. I am taking as much time on all of this training as they will give us. I am more anxious to get a thorough training than I am to get through fast. I realize that the better I train myself the more use I will be when I get into action. So you can rest assured that I will be careful and thorough in this work. This course is not very long, at most only about four weeks with good weather. I will have at least one more school to go to after this, though.

Russell is just about finished from all I can find out, and he will be down here very soon. I write to Russell and Alice about three times a week (almost) but I guess they are too busy to answer my letters. I hear from them through fellows who come from their school. I cannot get over to see them unless I go AWOL [absent without leave] and that is pretty risky business. Perhaps I can get over in a plane when I get further along here. They let some fellows do that, so here's hoping.

Yesterday evening, the 3rd, there was a big dance at the Red Cross. It was so crowded that we could not dance much, but we had an awfully good time. There were quite a number of girls from the neighboring Ys and Red Cross huts. Also some French people. We actually had ice cream, cake, and lemonade! That is one thing I think I missed more than anything else in the food line—ice cream. We have today, tomorrow, and the next day off as a 4th of July celebration. As there isn't much of any place to go I expect to stay here. The town has no attraction for me, outside of historic or beautiful places.

Thank heavens I had a wonderful bringing up. Dear Mother and all the rest of you, I can never be thankful enough for the ideals and morals you have given me. Too many fellows go to the bad over here and if I had not had such a Mother and Father and such brothers and sisters and such an Auntie, I might too. But believe me I am safe. What is pleasure to some is absolutely loathsome to me. Some fellows are over here for good (perhaps the better for them), [while] others will return but will be ashamed to meet their folks. But you can take my word that whether I stay or whether I return, I will have as clean a conscience and as pure a heart and body as when I came over. So if anything should happen to me just remember that you have less to grieve about than many people whose sons and brothers and sweethearts have returned to them.

Well I really must stop now as it is getting late. No added danger to life or limb suggested the subject of the last few paragraphs to me but only some conversation overheard last night. Love to you all, Percival

Letter, July 6. Dear Family: I am glad we start work again tomorrow. I have stayed here in camp, and though I have been able to do as I please I would rather work. Yesterday I wrote some letters and slept most all the morning. In the afternoon I took a bath and wrote more letters. The evening was much better. I wrote some more letters, watched a boxing match, and went to a YMCA dance. You see they even give dances in the Ys over here.

It was a fine dance too. There were really a lot of girls from the Canteens, the Red Cross, and the Hospital and it was not nearly so crowded as it was at the Red Cross dance. So you see your young son is having quite a gay time away over here in France.

I think I've told you before that you need not worry about me. I would not be any where else for anything. You don't know what it means to us to walk in the Canteen and see real American girls behind the counter. They are always smiling and cheerful. I am getting very anxious to see Alice again so I will try hard to work it somehow. Russ is about finished there but there are rumors that he may be sent to some other school. That school [St. Maxient] is a wonder so if he is sent there he will gain in training anything we might lose in not being together. Well I must stop and write to Alice. Love to each and every one of you dear ones. Percival

Letter, July 6. Dear Alice: As you know by now, I could not get over to see you during our three days leave over the 4th. I asked the Major about it but he said it was impossible. That meant that I would have to go AWOL if I went and as I had no orders to bluff with I thought I'd better not take a chance. I hope to get over in about two weeks in one of these planes. They let a few do that and if the Chief de Piece [Section Chief] knows you he may let me go. I have received the bad news that Russ has either gone to St. Maxient or to some other flying school; I have forgotten the name. The school in question is a wonder I understand, so if he has gone there he will be in luck even if we don't get together. I have got a new uniform in the process of construction and when it is done I will have to bring it over to have the brevette sewed on. Everything is going finely so don't worry. Lots of love, Percival

Letter, July 8. Dear Family: Well, once you get started in this school it doesn't take long to finish up. I have passed three fields and am on my way to the fourth tomorrow. We have a different type of work at each field. The next one we have will have a different and better machine. That is how we progress, by steps. We all had to take another physical exam, such as we had in New York on enlistment, before we could go on to the next field. I passed in perfect condition. The tests of spinning around were worse than before, but they could not make me sick. It pays to keep away from cigarettes and wine.

I have had almost a full day off today. I started by getting up at 5:15 and flying at 6:15. I finished on that field by 7:30 so I had nothing till the 2:30 physical exam. Then I am off till tomorrow at 5:15 again. They are beginning to realize that one needs plenty of time off during flying days, so we are getting it. As a result I can keep in fine health; I really never was feeling better.

I wish you could be with me for this evening. It is now 6:30 and I am sitting at a writing desk in the back room of the Y. There are about eight other officers reading or writing, in comfortable chairs or at nice tables. The walls of the little room are decorated with French posters of all kinds. Right in front of me is a large picture of a battle of the Marne from the 5th to the 12th of September 1917. Above it is a picture of a trench in a night attack on Champagne. At one side there is a picture of a Belgian woman working in a field with a lot of French under it that I can't make out. Outside, the airplanes buzz around in the sky, with the hum of wonderful power. I never will get used to watching them. I have been in this game for quite a while now, but whenever I hear one doing acrobatics I have to go out and watch. It is a wonderful sight to see them turning and twisting every way and never minding at all. These ships are so balanced that they always come out right straight as pretty as can be.

After I finish a couple of letters I will go in to the Canteen, get a cup of chocolate and some crackers, and have a little to eat. After that the movies start and last till about nine when I go to bed. I bought myself an alarm watch which is the pride of the barracks. It is just like a regular watch only you can set an alarm on it. The only trouble is that I now have the job of waking everybody up that flies at the same time that I do. Quite a proposition. I am keeping up my diary right along. Judging from the proportions it has already taken, I will have a six volume edition for sale at the end of the war—"My Four Months in France"—you see I expect the war to quit in four months. By that time the Kaiser will know I am here and will give up. Well I am expecting a bunch of mail soon. Love to all, Percival

Tuesday, July 9: I sure have not written in this for quite a while but I can remember everything that has taken place pretty clearly. Friday was a very poor day. I slept until after ten o'clock and then went to the Y to write letters. The afternoon was the same way only more letters. In the evening I watched a boxing match for a while until it was about time for the Y dance. I did not intend to go until I heard the music and saw everybody going. The temptation was too great. It was a mighty good party, though it was a little crowded.

Saturday I slept until late again and then wrote some letters. At 1:30 went downtown to get my pictures as Issoudun was to close up Saturday midnight. Sunday flying started at 6:15. Welty gave me a couple of rides and then let me go to the tester. Managed to get by this time and was put on 23 meter solo machines [Fig. 9]. I reported to that field (Field 3) right away but did not get up until afternoon. The 23 meter solo ships, or singles as they are called, are the same as the 23 meter doubles except that they only have one control. Woody and I stuck together again and are still together. We got up for a few rides and a half hour's air work that afternoon. We did not get back till 9:45 so we went right to bed.

Monday morning we reported to Field 3 at 6:15 and got a machine right away. We were both finished up by 7:30 but by then it was too late to take the required physical exam. We took the exam in the afternoon and passed without getting sick. It was about the same as we had in New York except a little more severe. It took in the spinning chair only. The rest of the day was nicer and I spent most of it sleeping. The movies in the evening were pretty good.

This morning Woody and I reported for 18 meter work at Field 9. We did not get up in the morning but managed to get in a half hour's air work and some landings in the afternoon. The air was awfully rough so I could not get much out of my air work. It was a little fun to be up in a new machine alone on a mighty rough day. We got back late pretty tired out.

Fig. 9. Nieuport 23, Issoudun, France (OHTM)

Letter, July 10. Dear Alice: I have just got your letter dated July 5th. I don't know what could have happened to the rest of your letters as this is the first word I have had from you or Russ since I left you about three weeks ago. I may be able to get up to see him sometime but I don't think he will be sent here. I am getting along finely so far. I am about half way through the flying and the rest ought not to take as long as what I've covered. I've not had any trouble of any kind as yet and I am being mighty careful not to have any. I took the required physical exam the other day and was pronounced in fine shape. I am being careful what I eat. I don't drink anything but coffee, water, and chocolate and I don't smoke; so there is no reason why I should not be able to keep in fine trim. That is half the game too, I believe.

It is a pretty bad day today, but as I got in all my flying before eight o'clock I am in luck. I have the rest of the day to rest up. I will probably get sent to [a] bombing [unit] before I get through here. But I would not mind much if I did as that is an awfully good way to start regular line work. I am mighty glad to hear that Russ is doing so well. To tell you the truth I do not worry about him anyhow. He can take care of himself and he will. My policy is to never worry about anything until you get some good reason and definite information. I think you'd better start that system, honey, or it will be too hard on you when we get further along. You have to be an absolute fatalist in this war. Well take care of yourself dear and don't worry about us. That is the only thing that wories your loving brother, Percival

Thursday, 11 July: Yesterday Woody and I finished up on 18s. We had a few more landings and some spirals. I got into three vrees [vrilles—spins] during my spirals but otherwise they went all right. They are lots harder to do on 18s than on Curtisses [Jennies]. The rest of the day I took off as I did not have to report out at Field 5 for 15 meter work. I went to bed early and got a good rest. This morning we packed up our stuff and moved to Field 5. Just before we left the main camp news came that Vorhees had been killed over on 18s. He was the next one on the list after Woody and me.

Field 5 is a pretty good place on the whole. The barracks are about the same only a little more crowded than the main field, the mess is fine, they have the good idea of putting you on your own responsibility, and the planes are wonderful. We had a class on the handling of Manettes [fuel controls] and a talk by the officer in charge of training and were then started off on the landing class. That consists of landing properly inside a circle. It is quite a job but not as bad as it is made out. The 15s are wonderful little machines. They were used at the front at one time for fighting with a little more powerful engine. We are flying 80s [80 horse power engines] at this field. Later we will have 120s. I wrote three letters (home, Russ, and Alice) and then went to bed.

Letter, 11 July. Dear Alice: I have passed the most difficult and dangerous part of my training now. You will just have to take my word for it as it is a perfectly well recognized fact around here. However don't imagine that I am going to be any the less careful. The idea is this—there has not been an accident at this field that has not been due to first carelessness or second boneheadedness. There have been almost no accidents in the work I am now in—because the fellows know how to be careful and use their heads, so don't worry. Of course there is always a good chance of breaking a ship a little or some rule and getting put out, but if things go well, I will be through in a couple of weeks. I am living at the field at which I am now flying. When I finish here I will move on again to the next one. As yet I have no bunk. Some of the fellows will move out tomorrow so it will be better. I will have to start looking for a "place to lay my head" pretty soon. I am also going to try to get in a letter home, so I'd better stop. Take care of yourself dear honey, and believe me I am being good. Love, Percival

Friday, July 12: I slept in the enlisted men's barracks last night as there were no bunks in this one. It certainly was funny at lights out and reveille to hear the old top sergeant swear at the men with no effect at all. We started flying in the "air work" class at about six thirty. Woody and I came about as close to getting killed as you can come and get away with it. I took off first and went straight ahead climbing as I went. Then Woody took off a little behind me and on my right. When I got over a certain road which was our limit, I turned sharply to the right. According to ruling Woody should have changed over to the left and of course I should have looked back but we were both at fault. The result was that when I looked around there was this machine coming right at me not 100 feet away. I jammed my stick over to the left and down and pushed on all my left rudder. The little ship almost jumped out from under me. She swerved up on one wing and down she went in a tight vrille. I only had 400 meters so I didn't waste any time. Without cutting my motor I shoved the rudder in neutral, pushed forward on my stick, and out she came. Woody missed me by a few feet only. I don't think he made a move. We were both pretty scared but we went on with our air work and finished up on our eights and Ss. The rest of the day was too windy and rainy to fly.

We had a class in Topography and one in engine repair. We shoot traps once a day and the rest of the time is ours. There was a fine concert in the Y and Miss Waters brought down the house with several simple little songs. Woody and I walked over to the main camp, about two miles, and stayed around for half an hour or so. Another fellow was killed today over in Field 8.

Letter, July 14. Dear Frank: I am driving small fast planes now—about as small as they come. They are wonderful! I never knew what it was to fly before. The planes are not nearly so dangerous as an ordinary Curtiss, because the powerful engine pulls you out of any trouble you might happen to get into. Also I am getting more sense of the air all the time and am getting the feel of the machine so well that I can handle it easily. Don't think for a minute that I am careless or overconfident. The further I go in this game the more careful I get.

I have never been in better shape in my life. The towns around here have very little attraction as there is nothing of much interest in or around them, so I get exercise walking over to the main camp and playing baseball. We have fine food and plenty of sleep so everything is perfect. I am going over to the main camp to see if Russ is possibly coming in this afternoon. There are some fellows to arrive from where he is but I am afraid he won't be in the bunch.

I've not been able to see Alice lately, in fact, since I came here, but I may be able to work it the next time I get my orders. Well, don't let the people worry about me as I am perfectly happy. Lots of love, Percival

Letter, July 14. Dear Alice: I am still on those little machines, but I have not got to the powerful ones yet. They are really a good deal safer than the machines I have already finished with. These are powerful enough to pull themselves out of anything you try to put them into. There is a mighty nice fellow here named Woody who was over at your camp all winter. He and I have been right together in everything we have done so far. We were in the same section to start with and we have gone through exactly the same classes ever since, right together. Well it is about time for church so I guess I had better stop here. Lots of love, Percival

Sunday, July 14: Yesterday we only got in a little flying in the afternoon. Just enough however to finish up on vrilles. The morning class was too crowded and so we could only practice on an old fuselage. The work went very well and as that was all we had Woody and I went over to the main camp. No baths however so we came home early. Sunday morning (this morning) I wrote some letters and went to church. After dinner I went over to the main camp to look up Russell. He came in late in the afternoon with Sam. I certainly was glad to see them again. Russ has evidently done some mighty good flying. I showed them all over camp and had a fine visit with them. Got back pretty late.

Tuesday, July 16: Yesterday was one of the stillest days I have had to fly yet. This 15 requires some wind to keep it from chevalling [ground-looping]. I had spirals to do and got through pretty well. In the morning I got in four and stopped in the circle three out of four times. Nothing broke too which was pretty lucky. Most of the ships were finally busted. Russ came over about 4 o'clock on his bike. We looked over our place and tried to keep cool. At six they started flying again. There was a big storm coming over by the main camp but I got in my two required spirals before it came too close. Went over to camp with Russ. He and Sam and I went for a walk up to the graveyard where there are now 44 graves (three last week) [Fig. 10]. Russ took some pictures of the yard and camp. There was a most marvelous cloud formation which the three of us watched for some time. Finally we ended up by going to a band concert and walking home.

This morning I started Aerobacy. First we went through virtual [practice] virages and renversements in an old fuselage on the ground. Later we went up and did them. It was a perfect day for flying, clear and a good breeze. Coates had a forced landing on the takeoff into some wheat. We thought he must be killed by the way his ship turned over but he only broke an arm. Woody and I got through everything except "side-slips" by 10:30. It was pretty good sport but a little too mechanical. When we got back to camp there was an order for me to report to the Assistant Adjutant. It scared me some but turned out only a bill of $1.50 at Park Field. I took dinner with Russ and Sam.

Loafed around all the afternoon until supper. After supper we went up and did our slide-slips. The first one I went over on my back and glided some distance that way. It was a great sensation. The next one was a good vertical slip of 400 meters. Great sport. Went over to the main field again, took a bath and visited with Russ till 10:00.

Letter, 17 July. Dear Fred: Russell arrived here Sunday last. You can bet I was glad to see him. He is just the same old fellow and now it seems as if he had never been away. I met him Sunday afternoon and spent the rest of the day with him and Sam. Though I am out at one of the outlying fields, I have managed to see him about twice a day. We generally get together in the evenings and have a great old time. I have finished the field I was at when I wrote last and am now at another one. From here I will go to a different school for about two weeks I expect. Work at this field just started this afternoon for me, but tomorrow I will get into it in earnest.

We fly about six hours a day in the fastest planes I have yet had. They are the same as I have been used to with a more powerful motor. For that reason (the motor) they are even safer than the

Fig. 10. American Aviators' Cemetery, Issoudun, France (OHTM)

others. The fact is the higher up you get in these schools and in Aviation the safer the planes and the flying. When we get to the front the Boche will be the only thing we need fear and of course everybody in the war is exposed to him. I have talked with Russell and have persuaded him to take his time and not try to catch up with me. I also showed him that he would have to be mighty careful not to break any rules nor try any stunts if he wanted to continue Aviation. They put you out if you break rules around here. You need not worry about him as no one gets hurt who is very careful and uses his head.

It is very hot here now. We have very funny little storms too. It just pours for a minute and then the sun comes out and everything clears up until the next shower. We don't even stop flying for these little wettings as they just cool us off and are perfectly harmless. There is a wonderful rain coming in just a couple of minutes now. It is after supper though so I don't care if it bursts a cloud. I am really having a wonderful time from morning till night. I feel quite conscience stricken. Love, Per

Letter, July 17. Dear Alice: Russ and Sam arrived at camp here Sunday. It certainly has been great to see them. I am out at one of the outlying fields but I get in to see them pretty often. Of course you have seen them within a week or two but they looked to me to be in fine health. I have talked to Russ and I can assure you he will be careful. You know they won't stand for any funny business here and if you are seen doing any, out you go. Russ understands this and I know he will be mighty careful. I am just as careful as I can be, because I know that the only ones that get hurt around here are hurt through their own carelessness or bone-headedness. I received three letters from home and two more today. They certainly are back of us every minute over there, and you can bet I am going to live up to their highest hopes and expectations. You should be glad, honey, that my getting hurt is the only thing you need worry about. Some people have lots worse worries than that. Thank Heaven the things some fellows are a slave to, do not tempt me at all. Take care of yourself honey and don't worry about your brother. Lots of love, Percival

Thursday, July 18: Yesterday I arrived over here at Field 7. It is a pretty nice place with about ten hangars, six barracks, a good Y, and a fine mess. We started by taking two little trips in the afternoon. The idea was to get used to flying and landing these 120 horsepower Nieuports. I started on a cross country for Romorantin but my oil wasn't working. Russ and Sam came over in the evening just in time to get caught by a terrible storm which wrecked some of the ships and hangars at Field 9.

This morning I took a trip to Romorantin and another to LeBlanc. One was about 80 kilos and the other about 120. The trips were very easy as France has clear landmarks. In the afternoon I had two formation flights. They were pretty hard work as you have to watch the man next to you every minute. I was the rear of a diamond formation. In the second one I was leader. We covered three hours flying in all. In the evening Woody and I wrote up our cross countries.

Letter, July 20. Dear Alice: This last week has been a great one. I am just about through Field 7 now, with only an altitude formation flight to make. The work here has been pretty hard but very good. We have been flying about six hours a day in formations which is about the most tiring flying possible. It has been so windy today that we had to call off flying at noon. As a result I've had a good rest, bath etc. I will probably be sent on to Field 8 Monday. After a few days there I will be sent to [Cazeau]. I see lots of friends of yours every day around here. I only wish you knew the Commanding Officer of our field. I tried to persuade him to let me take a ship to Tours but he would not consent. If I had some more drag I could have made it. There is no chance now, though. I suppose Russell keeps you posted on how he is progressing. He and Sam seem to be doing pretty well. If they keep up they will get through in great shape. Well honey I am having a wonderful time and everything is going just beautifully, so don't worry about us. Just take good care of yourself and all the boys at Tours. These boys over here will never forget what you have done for them. Your loving brother, Percival

Letter, July 20. Dear Family: My work has been going finely. I have learned more about flying in the last four days than I have ever learned before in a week. I have been flying cross-country and formations at the rate of six hours a day. Formation work is the best thing one can do to train himself to think, act, and move automatically. You see where you want your plane to be and you automatically maneuver it into place. That allows you to take your mind off your flying and put it wholly on the Boche. The work has been a little tiring, but that has been one of the best parts of the training. I now have one more formation [flight] to make to finish up on this field. It will be an altitude formation above 5000 meters and to stay up fifteen minutes. That really is not much of a test. I had two stunt formations today which were great sport. I led one of them. We have perfectly beautiful planes to do all this work in, which makes it a real pleasure instead of a drudgery. When I finish this field I will be sent to another school for a little while. I am having a wonderful time and everything is going just finely. I think I'd better stop now and look for Russ. Love, Percival

Sunday, July 21: The last few days of last week were pretty busy. Friday I had two two-hour formations in the morning and one two-hour formation in the afternoon. That certainly is tiring work. Unless you are leading the formation it is necessary to watch the plane next to you every minute and keep slowing down, speeding up, climbing or turning the whole while. It was a very hot day which did not tend to keep me very wide awake. Woody and I went in to the main camp more for the ride than anything else. I found Russ in the Red Cross writing letters and we had a few minutes together. The night before a Lt. Mason was killed in night flying. It was too bad as the course does not amount to a thing.

Saturday I was due to take my altitude formation but it was too cloudy. As a result I had two stunt formations of which I led one. They were quite interesting though a pretty heavy strain on the nerves as you had to watch pretty closely when the ships got all mixed up. We managed to get along all right though. In the afternoon it blew so hard that it was impossible to fly. I got a good hot bath and dressed up for the weekend. We got such a hard blow just after noon that it wrecked a good many of the ships out at Field 2 [Fig. 11]. I got a ride over to the field at the main camp on a YM truck. It busted down so it took me two hours to get there.

Russ and Sam were down town so I wrote letters home for a while. I stayed overnight at the main camp and slept over Russ. We did not get up until late and soon went to dinner. In the afternoon we walked over to Field 2 to see the ships that were busted up. It certainly was a shame. Russ took some pictures at different places which will be good if they come out.

Letter, July 22. Dear Old Al: I got your letter written on the 16th, 17th, and 18th of July this afternoon. If I had known that you were sick I would have swiped a ship and gone AWOL to see you. Not because I would have been worried about you but just because I could not stand having you sick all alone. As it was I went to the Commandant of the field to try to get a ship over the weekend. You must be all well by now and I hope you are at the "Hostess House" having a good and well-earned rest up. From what I hear from your friends you need it. Don't bother to write if you are too busy. Your old pal, Per.

Letter, July 22. Dear Father: I think I am writing home pretty often but they may not seem to you to come very regularly. I try to get in a letter home and one to Alice about every third day, but once in a while I miss one. As a result of the frequent exchange of mail there never is very much to say, especially when the censor rules cut out a good deal of the most interesting information. This time I am going to fool the censor (if this letter is re-censored) by giving only accounts of personal experiences.

After I left off talking to you last Saturday evening in my letter addressed to Auntie I went out to find Russell. As I expected, he was at the Y movies with Sam. As they were just about through we went out for a little walk around the camp to work up an appetite. I borrowed some blankets and slept in the upper bunk over Russell. He got up early to fix up his album but Sam and I slept on till late—too late for breakfast, in fact. After dinner Russ showed me his collection of little trinkets and pictures. Later we went out over

Fig. 11. Aircraft destroyed by wind damage, Issoudun, France (OHTM)

the camp to see what damage had been done by the wind of the Saturday before.

After supper I started home to this field. There was no chance for a ride so Russ came with me for the walk. You would have laughed to see your two sons trudging along a railroad track dressed up in old clothes with an old blue bag over shoulders (alternately). The bag contained my laundry. We remarked as we stumbled over the ties, "What if the famly could see us now?" Well, if you could, you would have seen two of the happiest sons you have got. It was a marvelous cool evening, a good six mile walk, long accounts of past experiences in France, plans for the future and never a care or a worry in the world. Oh, this is the life. Outdoors, sunburn, wind, rain, plenty of food and sleep; doing the thing you most prefer to do in the world and they call you a hero for doing your bit. Can you beat it? Of course, there is the other side, that we are taking a chance and we are far away from home and you all, but when we think of the cause it squares that up. Well as I was saying, Russ and I had a great old walk and talk.

When I did get to bed I slept with a vim that almost drowned out my alarm watch which pealed forth at five o'clock this morning. I got up in as big a hurry as my warm bed and sleepy condition would permit and got out all my warm clothes. It looked foolish as it was a hot day, but I had an altitude formation the first thing and they said it was cold up around the sun and stars. After breakfast I put on a very heavy sweater that Lu knit and a double-weight Teddy Bear suit like the ones Russ and Sam had on in their pictures. That, with a knit helmet and a pair of heavy gloves covered most of me up.

We started off in formation from the ground at 6:30 sharp. Up and up we went making large circles of about three miles in diameter. When we got to 4000 meters my altimeter busted, but on we went. The air was getting a little bit rare as we approached 5000 meters. We had to breathe more deeply and cut down the gas supply to our engines. At 5500 meters my barograph ran out of ink but I could still see the little marker going up. Finally the engines were wide open and the air did not give enough resistance to pull us up any more. The controls got kind of limp and did not respond very quickly. It was cold; cold as a zero day in winter I believe. My poor old sunburnt red sore face was about numb, my hands were awfully cold, and I could see the oil freeze on my little windshield. I took a last look at my barograph. The needle had run off the paper at 20000 feet. When I looked at the formation, the leader had peaked and we were on the downward stretch.

The country down below was perfectly beautiful. The forests of dark green were scattered around in great blotches with the grain fields in between like patches of vegetables in a truck garden with roads for dividing paths. As I glided down in slow easy spirals my engine popped and sputtered as any rotary will while idling. The noise would grow dimmer and dimmer until I swallowed and then there would be a big crack in my ears and I could hear the wires whistling again. My! but the warm air did feel good. It seemed to bring new life to my old altimeter and soon my barograph took to writing again. As we neared 2000 meters I watched the leader for the signal of dismissal from the formation. Exactly on the dot he dipped one wing and then the other and dove straight for the ground. The five of us scattered like so many children let loose from school, diving, zooming, spinning, slipping, and putting in a stunt now and then. Finally, one after another we glided into our field and taxied the little "bugs" up to the gas tank.

That finished me up on this field. Tomorrow morning I will be sent to Field 8 which is a little nearer the Main Camp where Russ is, I am glad to say. I don't know how long I will be there but it is all intensely interesting and very important work. Well, this is an awfully long letter and it has taken so long to write it that it is most bed-time now. I will have to get a cup of hot chocolate here at the Y and slip into bed. What do you think of our Sammies in this drive? The Germans may be able to stop bullets but they can't stop us. Your loving son, Percival

Wednesday, July 24: It has been quite a time since I wrote this up last. I have been so busy working at this new field. Monday I finished up at Field 7 by taking my altitude formation. It was mighty cold up about 5500 meters but I did not quite freeze. The air was pretty thin which affected my breathing somewhat. There was nothing else to do that morning or afternoon so I managed to get a ship for a half hour's air work. Tuesday morning I was shipped over here to Field 8. It is a pretty good place with plenty of flying, about five hours a day. The food is fine and we get plenty of sleep.

Wednesday I got my ship assigned to me, 478. It is a pretty good little fellow but I cannot virage it tight enough. The first period I did line of flight work. One fellow would fly straight ahead and the others would dive at him from all angles. The next period they gave us air balloons and we were to let them loose and dive at them as they sank. When I let mine go I pulled up into a stand and fell into a vrille. Needless to say I did not see my balloon again. I got into a couple of combats and got ridden pretty well. The machine gun class was full, but I managed to take another fellow's place [Fig. 12]. In the afternoon period I took seven line of flight pictures. After I had finished I got into two combats and got ridden around again. Perhaps after I get more time I may be able to ride some myself. Went to bed early after writing Alice and home.

Letter, July 24. Dear Alice You Old Honey: I'll bet that no other three brothers and sister get together over here as we have. We might be scattered all over France but instead here we are right together—almost. I see an awful lot of Russ even though this field I am at now is some 10 minutes from the main camp, where he is. This is the last field that I go through here. After this I have a little course at another school, and then I am going to try to get somewhere where I can get a lot of flying, combat and formation work. This work is mighty interesting though it is pretty tiring. Still we only get four hours a day with good rest periods between—so it isn't bad at all. They treat us wonderfully at this field too. Fine food, good quarters, and plenty of rest. We each have a ship of our own which we use all the time. I am crazy about mine and treat it as carefully as possible to keep it in good shape. I've got a couple of good mechanics too, who look after everything and take great pride in keeping the ship looking and running well.

It really isn't very risky flying here at this school. Certainly no more than at any other. It is just necessary to cut out fooling and get down to serious work. That is what I have done and it is what

Flying Training

Fig. 12. Percival Gates and Gunnery Range, Issoudun, France (OHTM)

Russ is doing. The only fellows who get hurt, get hurt through carelessness. I think I have said that before but it is proven true every time we have an accident. This combat flying is about as safe as they have here, as you have your eye on your opponent every minute and everyone here can maneuver a ship so well that there isn't much chance of accident. Also all our work is done at high altitude. None of this contour [low-flying] stuff in this place. I'd better stop now as I have one more letter to write. Your loving brother, Percival

Letter, July 24. Dear Mother: I am at the last field of this school now; from here I will be sent to a different place. The work here is very interesting and of the highest importance. Here we do actual fighting and maneouvering using camera guns. You have to pass an examination before you can graduate, so there is no danger of my being sent through and to the front without being properly trained. There is a chance that I will flunk the exams, of course, in which case I will go [to] bombing, or something like that. The exam consists of a combat with one of our instructors. I never knew the true meaning of having a "Hun on your tail" until this afternoon. Of course it wasn't a regular Hun, but he was an old flyer and he certainly did stick to me in spite of anything I could do. In a couple of days I will be able to do that to someone else. At present I am just learning, but as we get four hours a day it won't take long to get on to the knack of it.

I had the most beautiful ride this morning; there was a thick blanket of clouds at about 1500 meters. It did not take me long to get above them. Large billowy clouds with deep caverns and caves in them. It reminded me of a prairie covered with ten feet of snow with the snow heaped up in beautiful mounds over the rough ground. Finally the clouds seemed to break up a little and form into great high mountains of fleece. It was great to dodge in among them, climb over the top, and dive through them leaving a perfectly round hole behind where you came through. It is impossible to describe what goes on in the air—one has to see it for himself and experience it. I took some pictures which may show something.

The driving of the plane comes perfectly naturally now. In

such work as we are doing now it is impossible to put any attention on running the machine. You have to watch your sparring partner all the time. You think your plane into a certain position and it just goes there. This sounds like a rather wild letter but this is really the safest work I've done yet. These are beautiful machines and we have all had enough flying to know what we are doing and how to keep perfect control. I see Russell about every day, for a while at least. Yesterday it rained and I was with him all the afternoon and most of the evening. Well I must stop now. Your loving son, Percival

Friday, 26 July: Yesterday was the same thing over again—line of flight in the first period, machine gun lecture, balloon diving, and fixed target in the afternoon. There were some wonderful clouds that were great sport to play in. I chased a fellow all around, in and out, through holes, and down into caves and caverns. I did a little better in my combat and managed to shake one fellow and get on his tail. I went over to the main camp and saw Russ fly in the evening. He did pretty well and is certainly trying hard enough. I got home pretty late on the liberty truck.

This morning I had some more line of flight pictures. Of the whole film only five came out but all of them were hits [Fig. 13]. There were some more wonderful clouds up there of which I got some pictures. I went up 3500 meters with a balloon filled with air the second period. Unfortunately just as I was about to let it go it busted. I spiralled, vrilled, and barrelled till I got down again. It was awfully rough in the afternoon period and rained most of the time. Unfortunately I had to dive at fixed targets. As a result I could not get more than 100 meters which is pretty low on a rough day. There was a most beautiful rainbow which made a complete circle around my plane. I never saw one just like that before. I wrote some letters and went to bed early.

Letter, July 26. Dear Auntie: I am now in the Red Cross rest room. That is not an infirmary or anything like that, but just a Red Cross place that corresponds to the YMCA, with magazines, music, and writing tables. I had to go to the machine gun lecture and when I got back I was so tired I slept for two hours before going

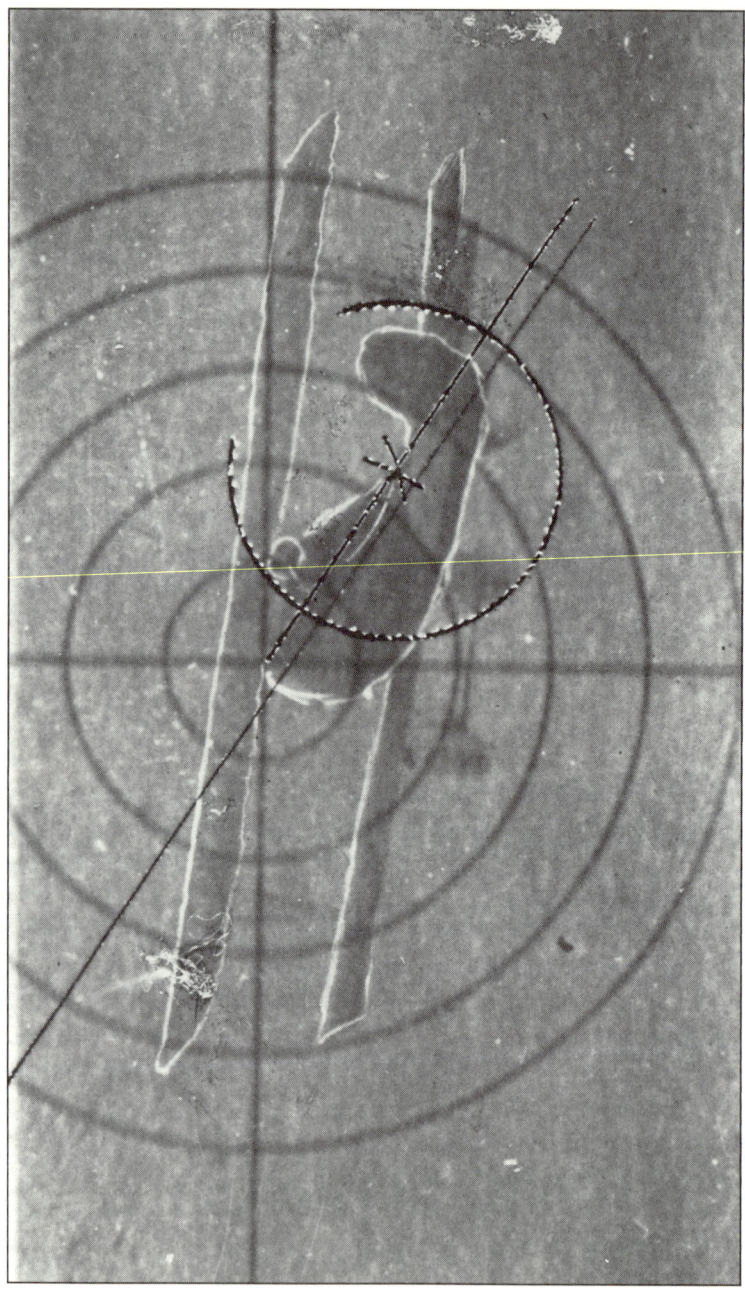

Fig. 13. Image from Percival Gates' Gun Camera Film, Issoudun, France (OHTM)

on my last flight at 4:00 PM. My work this afternoon consisted of flying around the field and diving down at white targets of aeroplanes on the ground. Whenever I got a good shot at one I would take a picture of it with my camera gun. When the film is developed I will be able to tell if I would have hit my mark if I had been shooting bullets. We use the same camera gun in all our combat work.

After I had practiced diving and taking pictures for about an hour I climbed up through a hole in the clouds, way up on top of them all. After flying around for a little while I got into a fight with another plane. We worked at shooting at each other for about ten minutes and finally quit by mutual consent. The combat work is lots of fun but pretty tiring as you have to keep maneuvering every minute. It is interesting to watch two fellows dive, turn, zoom (shoot straight up), climb, and slide down sideways. They look for all the world like a couple of birds fighting. Of course they are so high up that it is easy to get out of any possible trouble. We generally combat at about 2000 meters which you can see is considerably over a mile high.

We had a fine supper of pork, fried potatoes, lettuce, coffee cakes, bread (white—always), and butter. I believe we can get more over from our YM than you can buy in the states. My friend Woody is still with me. I hope we will go to the next school together. The chances are that some of us will go within the next two days. I must stop now, but just remember that I am perfectly happy. Love, Percival

Letter, July 26. Dear Old Al: I got over to see Russ for a couple of hours last night and saw him fly. He is doing very well and trying awfully hard. I have no fear of his trying anything foolish in the way of stunts. We get four hours a day of pretty hard combat work here. If it were not for the fact that we get good food and plenty of sleep, it would be hard to keep going. As it is, everything goes smoothly. I had a great time flying above the clouds today and I was in hopes that I would get lost and have to come down in Tours. Unfortunately the wind blew me right back home. I guess I will have to wait till the wind is blowing in the other direction. I will probably be sent away from here for about three weeks in a few days—if I am sent at all. The chances are pretty good that I will go bombing as they pick out the chasse men *very* carefully. Only a small percent get by. I would not mind at all as that branch is about the most interesting of all. I may choose it anyhow if I do finish here all right.

Russ has a good deal more Dual Control to go through before he gets really started. Once you get off DC things go pretty fast. I wish we could get together somehow but I don't see how that will be possible. The only way I could wait for him would be to bust something or to disobey a rule—and of course I could not do either one willfully. I guess I'd better stop and get a good *hot shower* before bed. Your loving brother, Percival

Letter, July 27.   Dear Cousin Helen: I guess you will be home by the time this letter gets to Texas, so I am addressing it to TCU [Texas Christian University]. I am still at the 3rd Aviation Instruction Center, but I will not be here much longer. I have gotten through my preliminary training and am now doing combat work in small fast fighting planes. I thought I knew how to fly when I was in the states but this work shows me that I didn't know much about it. In this combat work we climb, turn, flop over on our sides, back or tails, shoot straight up into the air and turn over and over in a barrell spin. It is great sport, but if you have any tendency to get sea-sick you'd better learn some other game. It gets to me once in a while but I guess I can stick it out. In order to get good practice in shooting we use camera guns. That is, we take a picture at the second that we would have pulled the trigger if we had been fighting Huns. It is very interesting to watch two fellows going at it way up in the sky. It looks like two great big birds fighting. Love to all, Percival

Sunday, July 28:   We had a big rest up yesterday. It was too rainy and windy to fly so we had the whole day off. However we had to stick around until afternoon to make sure that it would not clear up. We had a fine lecture on some of the things a chasse pilot should know. It looks to me like a pretty big job. I am going to stick to it if I can though. Russ and I took the liberty train to Issoudun at 7:00. He had some errands which did not take long and then we had a good meal. Fortunately we got a truck home.

This morning we did not get up until late and then only at the threat that the Major was coming through to inspect. We wrote some letters and Russ finished up his diary in the morning. We took some pictures of the barracks and target range in the afternoon. Russ, Sam, "Mitch" and I went for a walk out to Paudy taking numerous pictures on the way. We then [went] over an old town over there which at one time was a pretty strongly fortified place with a high wall, moat, and watch towers on the corners. From there we went over to my friends of the Chateau and found them playing tennis. We only stayed a few minutes but got a very cordial invitation to return next Sunday.

On the way home we stopped in at Paudy and got supper. It was a pretty good meal with jam omelet, chicken, bread and butter. Walked home slow in a wonderful evening through really glorious country. The grain has just been cut and the golden fields are covered with little stacks set in beautiful lines. Near the end of the field there are generally a couple of stacks where the grain on the stalks is piled. They leave it that way till the thresher comes through the country. I caught the liberty truck home and climbed in bed with a bunch of mail to read in the morning.

Letter, July 29. Dear Fred: This is going to be a short note as it is getting late and I am pretty tired. However, I cannot let this day go by without writing home, as my letter is due. They have cut our [flying] time down to three hours a day from four, so it is much better. We really can do better work for not being so tired. I am getting on to the idea of this combat work pretty well, but I still have an awful lot to learn. I don't know as yet whether or not I will be chosen for chasse work in the final test. As far as I can see the choice does not amount to much as you are liable to be sent bombing or contact patrolling or artillery observing or most anything when you finish. Well, I must stop. Love to you all, Percival

Letter, 30 July. Dear Old Al: I missed a day writing to you as I was very tired and did not have pep enough to write more than the one letter home last night. I am so glad you are at the Hostess House where you can get a good rest. I hope you are still there. You are due to have about two weeks off I think and if you can find any place to go or anyone to go with, I would take some time off if I were you.

Russ seems to be getting along pretty well with his flying. He will have to take more time than I did as he did not have so much at Tours as I did at Park Field. My work has been going fairly well, but I can tell you I am no such flyer as you have heard. I had an idea I was fairly good till I came to this field. Now I find I'm rotten. Perhaps I set my ideals too high and judge myself too severely, but I do know I have lots of work to do yet. I have a very good hunch that I will be sent bombing before long. I certainly will unless I can show more in the way of combat work. I've been pretty successful lately but I have not had a fight with the instructor yet. I would not mind bombing much. In fact I think that is a very good way to start work over the lines. Lots of love, Percival

Letter, July 31. Dear Father: This is the big summary report on my mental, moral, and physical condition along with a list of my letters received from home and the condition of my pocket book. I will try to get in one of these the last day of each month. First. I think I am perfectly sound mentally. That is, I am as well off in the way of brains as I have ever been. I still am perfectly happy to be here and though it would be a marvellous dream to be home, there is work to be done, and I could not be happy at home with this war unfinished. Whenever I think of you all and the grand times we could all have together, I can always dispel any signs of homesickness by the thought "apres la guerre [after the war]." My experiences in this country, my self-support and independence, my contact with the people and their customs and ways, have given me a broader outlook on the world and life than I could have got in several years of college and business life.

Second. I am just the same morally as I was when I left you all on the 21st of May. I have not smoked yet nor touched a drop of even the lightest wine, beer, or anything else. The greater evils have no attraction for me whatsoever, you need never worry about that.

Third. I have never been in better physical condition. As long as I have been in the service now, I have never been to the hospital nor have I had to miss a day's work or flying. I am training as carefully now as if I was working for the tennis team. As a result I never get spells of indigestion, which absolutely knocks out an Aviator temporarily. I never have any sign of dizziness or sea-sickness in the air. In other words, my system seems to be working pretty well so far.

Fourth. I have received during July one letter from Mother dated June 18th; three letters from Auntie dated June 9, 16th, and 18th; one letter from Frank dated June 14; three from Lucia, June 18th, 24th, and 30th; and three from Grace, June 12th, 18th, and 30th. Well that covers about everything for the monthly report. I will try to get in a letter about every other day if I can. Love to you all, Percival

Friday, August 2: I am so poor at keeping up this diary, I almost feel like quitting it. However, I will catch up once more and see if I can't take a brace. Monday we just had a regular flying day. It was my first day on actual combat work. I did not realize how much that could take out of you. However, after three hours of it, I was absolutely all in. We go out in parties of three and meet over a designated town. On the way somewhere we meet with another patrol of the enemy. We each pick a man and start combatting. In this work you dive at each other, zoom, virage sharply, turn in half-vrille turns, loop, barrell, or pull a renversement. Anything you can do to get your camera gun on your opponent and keep him from getting a clean shot at you.

Tuesday I had a great experience and at the same time a pretty close shave. I was combatting with a very good flyer. We started right for each other head on. I had the sun at my back so he could not see me well. My windshield was covered with oil so I could not see much and on we came. Just as I was about to snap my camera I looked up and there he was just ahead of me coming straight on still. I gave my stick an awful jerk. Up I shot into the air like a bullet, then there was a crash, [and] my plane settled and nosed over, trembling as she fell. That was one awful minute. Over to one side the fellow I had collided with was gliding down on an even keel. He was all right so I took a look around to see what had happened to me.

My plane had got up speed now so I had some control, but she was very heavy on the right wing and seemed to spiral that way. I looked out that side and saw the cause of my trouble. My right wing had been hit and six of the ribs had been broken. That bulged the end of the wing up so badly that she could not fly much. I corrected for it with my ailerons and managed to get down all right. It was a closer shave than I want again, especially in training. I got another ship—404—in the afternoon and went on with my work but being a little more careful.

Wednesday I had pretty hard luck. After my first period of one hour combat was over, I started for the field. Something was wrong with the motor and my left foot was very cold. I looked down and there the gas tank connection was busted and gasoline was pouring all over my feet. I cut her off and glided down to the main field. The field service fixed my machine while I visited with Russ and Sam. That was pretty good luck. I got back just in time to get in the afternoon's flying period.

Thursday I had worse luck still. I came down from my first period with one breather pipe just about out, the engine was backfiring into the fuselage, there was something the matter with the rudder post, and the elevators were jammed so that I could go up but not down. I had to cut my power to get into the field. I was pretty sore and told the mechanics what I thought about it. They had simply neglected the plane. The noon period I got old 393 which was all right except that she could not virage either way, climb, or loop. I tried to combat but it was almost hopeless. In the afternoon I got 329. That was a good ship for flying but the motor shook too much. It busted my camera gun and almost shook my plane to pieces. However, I had four combats and got the best of all but one.

The little plane could loop, too, better than any I was ever in before. I finally tried to loop over the field just before coming down. I got two loops and then the motor quit. I had to come down with a dead stick. Thus ended my last day of combat at

Issoudun. I walked over to the main field and spent the evening with Russ.

Friday (today), it rained off and on from six AM to ten tonight. As a result we did not have any flying. I loafed around most of the morning, writing up my diary, shaving, and attending classes including an exam in ring sights. This afternoon I wrote letters and slept with emphasis on the sleep. Woody left this morning for Orly. He had to go bombing and he took a last chance at chasse by going up there. He certainly is a good fellow and a hard worker. I am mighty sorry to lose him.

Russ has been talking a good deal with me about trying to kill time for three or four months and wait till the spring drive. It sounds good and there is no doubt but that it would greatly increase my chances of getting through. However, I came over here to do my duty not shirk it. Somebody has got to go to the front this fall and take what is coming to them. I would rather wait, but when they say I am ready to go I will go. I am no better than the next fellow and there is no reason why I should wait. I have finished my work at this field and this school. While I am awaiting orders for Cazeau I will try to fly the other planes we have here.

Letter, August 2. Dear Old Al: My work has been going finely lately. The combat work which was so hard at first is now a good deal easier. Of course the practice that I have had lately would be bound to show some result. However I have been a little more fortunate than some of the rest and have gotten through with my course here and made Chasse. I am feeling quite good about it as only about 20% of the men who come here to this school finish up as Chasse men. I don't know how good I am compared to the average green men at the front, but if they think at this school that I will make good I am willing to trust their judgment. However, you can be sure I'll never miss an opportunity to improve myself and I will never get to the point when I will be satisfied with my work.

Now I am awaiting orders to Cazeau which will probably come through very soon. In the meantime I will have a chance to fly some of the other types of machines that we have here. My course at C[azeau] as far as I can find out will take about a month. Then I will be sent to Orly where I will spend two or three months. Thus you see I will not be in action for at least three or four months. That ought to bring me in on the big spring clean-up. However that is a long way off and there is no use thinking or worrying about it.

Russ is coming along finely in his work. He has got out of Dual Control so he will go along pretty fast. From what his instructor has said about him he must be a very good flyer. The main thing is that he is trying awfully hard for Chasse and he is not taking the slightest chance on anything for fear of being sent bombing. He is taking this game more seriously anyhow, as we all do when we come to this field. We are training for our work at the front, the same as the Infantry or Artillery trains for its work. If we have to go up there you must think that we are doing no more than the ordinary buck private—merely our duty. As far as the danger of getting hit is concerned, I would not trade places with any man in the trenches.

My friend Woody has been sent bombing as he was a little too slow for Chasse. Don't say anything about it to his friends at Tours as he was quite disappointed. Well, honey, I must stop now; take care of yourself and don't worry about us, as your work demands all the strength you have. Your loving brother, Percival

Saturday, August 3: After breakfast I went out to see if I could get in some rides in the other types of machines. I found that the Spad was busted but that I was on the list for the Moraine and the Sopwith Camel. I took up the Moraine first. It was a little monoplane with a 120 horsepower Le Rhone [engine] in it. I had a hard time getting her off the ground as she was so fast and I could hardly reach the rudder bar. When she took to the air though she was a perfect dream. I have never driven a ship that flew so fast, so smoothly, so easily, and so perfectly. No matter what you did with her she was as easy to control as a plane could possibly be. I banked up vertical, looped, side-slipped, spiralled, vrilled, barrelled, and renversemented. Everything was a perfect dream. When I landed she came down along the ground at about ninety miles an hour but

Flying Training

she sat down on all three as easily as could be. I only hope I will have a ship like that at the front.

The next one I took up was the Sopwith Camel. It is a biplane with very broad wing, a short tail, and very small controls. It has a 130 [horsepower] Clerget rotary motor in it. The machine ran very well and with some practice and time, it would be pretty easy to fly. I did everything I could think of with it and finally tried to fly it on its back. It did very well. I looped it and on the top of the loop I pushed forward on the stick thus holding it on its back. It flew for a minute or two and then the engine stopped for lack of gas. The second time I tried it the engine quit altogether and I could not get it started again. As a result I had to come into the field with a "dead stick." The ride on my back was quite interesting; at first it is hard to do as the aileron and elevator controls work just opposite from the way they do when you are right side up.

The flying of those two planes finished me altogether, and I went to the barracks and packed up. We (five of us) started for the main field right after dinner where I put in an application for a pass to Limoges. I rode out to 18 meter Field 9 where Russ was on his bicycle. We waited around there for some time during several rainstorms. Finally after dinner they let us go home in a truck. I just had time to get dressed and catch the 7:00 train for Issoudun with Russ. After a long and hard assault on the house of L. Revard, who had some pictures for Russ and who was closed for the night, we gave up and got something to eat. Russ left for the main camp shortly afterwards while I waited for the 11:00 train for Limoges.

Sunday, August 4: I caught the 11:00 all right last night with two other fellows. There was not even room to sit down on it for at least an hour so we stood. At Chateauroux we got seats and from there on I was lost to the world. Some of the Frenchmen in my compartment knew that I wanted to get off at Limoges and they woke me up in time. We three pulled into a station at 3:30 AM which was jammed with people. I believe most of France travels at night. We made our way to the Red Cross Canteen and managed to get a hearing from a lady who was serving. She was an American lady who was on the night shift serving food to the poor soldiers,

French and American, who were passing through the station. She showed us to a little officers' room which contained about ten beds neatly made up with sheets, pillow cases, and blankets. That is the first real bed I have slept in since I left the boat almost three months ago. As I lay there just before I dozed off I thought of the talk Father gave us on the Red Cross just before I left and I thought I would tell him in my next letter where some of his money went.

I slept right through my alarm watch and only woke with the violent shaking of one of my friends at eight o'clock. After a fast dressing and washing and a cup of coffee, I started for Base Hospital 13 which was the goal of my wild trip. I found the hospital and in it I had no difficulty in locating Bernadine Fennelly, one of the nurses I knew on the boat and at Brest. She was on duty at the time but one of her friends relieved her so we went for a walk through the town. I had a wonderful time talking over our trip across and everything we had done together at Brest and what we had each done in the meantime. Anyone outside the Army and outside of France cannot possibly appreciate what it means to have lady friends over here. Especially when they are just like sisters. That is the way most of the American girls are who come over here.

My visit was not very long as I had to catch the noon train back to Issoudun. However it was a very successful trip in every way. Coming home I got into the dining car. It was quite [a] curious system. We sat down and found a pile of about six plates in front of each place. Then they brought on the food and served it out of one plate to each person. It was a fast system and worked out pretty well. The trip the rest of the way was wonderful, through mountains and valleys. I got home only too soon. I got Russ' pictures and a little something to eat and took the train home. I have been writing this up for the last few minutes and at last Russ has come back from Field 9. He has finished there and goes to Field 5 tomorrow. I have got the news that I go to St. Jean tomorrow.

Monday, August 5:   This is really Tuesday afternoon and I am on the train from Tours to Nantes. As it is a local I expect to have plenty of time to write. This is the first chance I have had to write up yesterday's doings. I spent Sunday night with Russ and Sam. Monday morning I had a little visit with Major Spatz* (Commanding Officer of the Post). He spoke to all ten of us about getting the most out of the work at St. Jean. The rest of the morning was spent in packing, settling up accounts, and arranging for mail forwarding. My truck was to leave for the train at 3:00. It was delayed however by the funeral of one of our aviators. I am not superstitious but it did seem curious that the first thing I saw when I came to Issoudun on June 18 was the funeral of a nurse and the last thing I saw as I left on August 5 was the funeral of an aviator. With that in mind it was hard to say good-by to Russ. I don't know when I may see him again for you can never tell.

Our train left at 5:30 for Vierzon, where we had to change. Some of the fellows stayed there overnight but I was determined to go to Tours. My train there was late and it was fully ten o'clock before I finally climbed aboard my little crowded coach. There was not a seat to be had so I stood up with some doughboys who were returning to their outfits after a three-weeks' stay in the hospital at Limoges. They had been wounded in the July 15th attack and their account was very interesting. It was a long stand but after two hours of it I got a seat. I only had half an hour's use of it when we pulled into Tours. I managed to get a room or rather a bed in a room at the YM Hotel. The sleep was mighty refreshing.

PART 4

Gunnery School, St. Jean de Monts, France, 7 to 25 August 1918

[His training at Issoudun completed, Gates next attended gunnery school at St. Jean-de-Monts, located on the west central coast of France, from 7 to 24 August. Gates' class of ten students was the first group trained at the newly-established school. The gunnery school at St. Jean was run by Americans, and had been set up to alleviate pressure on the French-run school at Cazeau. At St. Jean the students flew 15 Meter Type 22 Nieuports with 120 horsepower Le Rhone engines, although Gates also flew a Sopwith Camel on two occasions. Gates suffered his first serious crash at St. Jean when he tried unsuccessfully to fly a previously disabled Camel off the beach. However, gusty winds and damaged wing spars adversely affected the controllability of the aircraft, which landed abruptly immediately after takeoff in the shallow water offshore.

At St. Jean the students fired at fixed targets on the ground, including silhouettes and tethered balloons, and at targets towed behind other aircraft. During his seventeen days at St. Jean, Gates flew a total of approximately ten hours and completed the course with outstanding scores. He performed so well in the school that he was asked to stay on as a gunnery instructor, but he turned down the invitation, preferring to work towards an assignment at the front. At this point, Gates' school training was complete, and he was ready for an assignment to a combat unit.]

Tuesday, August 6: Once more I am a day late in writing this up but it is quite excusable as I got to Nantes at something after ten and had to go right to bed. The bed at Tours was so comfortable I almost did not wake up when my alarm watch went off at 7:00 AM. However, I did make it and had a good breakfast at the Y Hotel. I did not have to hunt very long to find a cab that would take me out to Alice's camp. I found her working at the center as happy and cheery as ever. She looked in such perfect health that you would never guess she had been sick. Needless to say she was mighty glad to see me as I was to see her. She seemed quite tickled to hear that I had made chasse. One of the French workers relieved her from duty so the dear old honey and I had a fine visit. Finally I had to leave to catch the 1:35 train for St. Jean-de-Monts. When I got to town it started raining so I bought a much-needed rain and fall overcoat combined. It cost me 275 francs but if I get to use it for some months I will get my money's worth out of it.

I met the other nine fellows at the station but only two of them took the same train I did. The three of us had a very slow and somewhat tiresome trip to Nantes. We did not get there until after ten and then we found that our train for Challans left at 5:00 the next morning. We got two beds in the Hotel de France. Another fellow and I slept together and we certainly slept the sleep of the just.

Wednesday, August 7: We had to get up and out at 4:00 this morning to catch the 5:00 train for Challans which was the only decent one we could take. The ride was very slow and tiring though I slept most of the time. A truck met us at the train and after we had a little breakfast took us to the camp. We are located right on the sea coast about two miles from the town of St. Jean-de-Monts. The field has been leveled off and cleared pretty well. A couple of months ago they say it was all forest. I walked out to the beach, wrote letters, and slept most all the afternoon. I am not feeling too well this evening. A long walk on the beach helped some.

Letter, August 7. Dear Frank: On the 1st of August I had my last ride, or rather work, at Issoudun. That finished me up and I graduated as a chasse (pursuit, in American) pilot. At last I had finished the school where "many enter in, but few reside." What I mean to say is that very few go all the way through the school. Most of the men are sent [to] bombing [school] during the course. I managed to get a ride in several different types of machines that were on hand. They were all monoplace fast machines, but I did not have any trouble running any of them. The machine I have been training in is the hardest of all to run.

I got a pass for Limoges and went down on the evening train. I got down there very late at night but found that there was a Red Cross rest room just across from the station. I went over there and was shown into a room with about ten beds in it for officers. They were small beds but they had sheets, pillow cases, mattresses, blankets and springs. Oh my! It was the first time I have seen such things since I left the boat. As I crawled in and started to doze off I thought of the discussion Father and I had about the value of the Red Cross and I said to myself I will have to write home and tell Father where some of his money has gone. Almost every large station has a Red Cross Canteen which is open day and night. Thousands of poor tired soldiers who have been traveling for days at a time get a chance to get off the train and have a cup of hot coffee and some kind of sandwich. If they cannot pay they don't have to. I got back to Issoudun Sunday afternoon after a very pleasant visit with some of my friends of the 13th Base Hospital unit, who came over with me on the boat.

Russ was still flying but he came in after supper and we went to the movies. Russ finished up with that field and has gone on to the little planes. He is a very good flyer from what his instructors tell him. I spent Monday arranging my affairs, reporting to various offices and officers, packing and saying good-by. At three I started for town in one of the trucks with some others. We took the train at 5:30 for Vierzon. The others stopped there a while but I went on to Tours to see Alice.

I found Alice sitting behind her counter, just as cheery and happy as ever. She showed no sign of having been sick and really looked much rested out. Of course she got relieved and we had a wonderful visit for two or three hours. She spoke of taking a leave for ten days or two weeks and I think she will do it all right. She is looking in fine health though, and the only reason she would take the leave would be because she had been so long at work without one and this seems an opportune time before winter comes on. I had to leave about noon to get dinner and catch the afternoon train for Nantes. The trip was through beautiful country, right through the Loire valley. I enjoyed it very much.

At Challans we were met by a truck and brought here to this Aerial Gunnery School at St. Jean-de-Monts. It is a peach of a place, all new and nicely fixed up. The main feature is that it is right on the coast. The ocean is just the other side of our field, not five minutes walk from our barracks. Oh! don't you wish you were spending a couple of weeks at the sea-shore? I've told you you would have to go some over there to have as good a time as I am having here. As I just arrived I know nothing of the school itself or the course, but it looks good to me so far. Swimming every day, plenty of time to oneself, lots of sleep and good food. This is too good to last. Well I must stop now as my luggage has come and I have to fix up my bunk. Love to all, Percival

Thursday, August 8: I had a bad night last night. About two o'clock I woke up awfully sick. I managed to get out of the barracks but that was about all. It was raining which did not help any as my pajamas are not waterproof. From then on till morning I had pretty frequent spasms of exercise. I did not eat any breakfast and stayed in bed until ten. Then at dinner I was not able to eat anything. As a result, I was feeling awfully low all the day. This evening however I am a little better off. I think what made me sick was the stuff I ate on the way here and the long train ride. I got all my baggage and things straightened out. Went to a Y concert this evening and then to bed. I hope I can get some good sleep tonight.

Friday, August 9: I was feeling much better this morning, so everything went finely. We had a couple of lectures on deflection and the Vickers gun this morning which took up all our time. Then we had a little shooting too which did not amount to much. The bullets ricocheted into some hangars so we had to quit. We had a couple more classes in deflection and machine gun in the afternoon. I have had all the stuff before but I don't think you can get too much of it. Everybody that comes from the front says "learn your gun and your sights." We had a great old swim in the ocean after classes. The water was warm and the sun was hot. There is a long beach here that is wide enough to land on if necessary. In fact, it is one of the best landing places when the tide is out.

I wrote some letters in the evening and then went for a long walk on the beach. It was certainly beautiful down there. The water was dark blue except for a long stretch of gold and red over toward the west. It was about eight thirty so there was no one else on the beach or in swimming. As I walked along all by myself thinking of a thousand different things and wondering what the next two months would bring, I cannot say I was exactly homesick, but more lonely—lonely for some old friend to talk to. There aren't many fellows here and most of them start for town right after supper. There is nothing of interest there for me so I prefer to walk on the beach.

Letter, August 9. Dear Alice: This is a nicely located place but as it is new it is not very well equipped or organized as yet. We are living in very nice little barracks with the ocean just across the field from us. It is only about a five minute walk to the most beautiful beach and all the swimming one could want. St. Jean is a very small town. The country around here is so much like northern New York that it fair makes me homesick. It is rugged, hilly, covered with low sand dunes and sage brush. There aren't many places to land but we always stay near home.

We started work this morning with some lectures. It will be several days before we fly. My first night here was a rather unfortunate one. I had been so careful of what I ate at Issoudun that when I began to move around and eat anything and everything I naturally got sick. I had a lively time during the night but I was better by morning. I took it easy the next day and did not eat much. As a result I am all right again today. This is only to be a short little letter to say I am here and everything is going well. I have a class pretty soon so I must stop. Lots of love, Percival

Saturday, August 10: We had a couple more classes in the morning on machine gun and deflection. In the afternoon Major Benedict and Major McGill joined our class. They will take the course with us. We went out on the range and had some shooting. Major Benedict talked at length on the different types of planes at the front and the tactics used in fighting. It is a cinch that the game is to be a good shot and get your man at a distance. That is the way all the Aces do. The men that close with the enemy don't last long as a rule.

The more I learn about this game and the more I hear about what our boys are doing up there in the trenches the more anxious I am to get in to the fight and drive those d--- Huns out. I almost wish I were in contact patrol so I could dive on them and help break up their retreat. I must admit, I don't expect to last long at the front. I am too anxious to kill those Germans. However, I have no complaint coming as the doughboy Second Lieutenant only lasts a few days. I am no better than he is. So when they tell us here that we only have a month to go at the front it doesn't trouble me much. I am here to give everything if necessary.

I went to town in the evening more for the ride down in a Fiat than anything else. After leaving some films to be developed and printed, I walked home along the beach. There was nothing to the town, only a few trinket shops, a store or two, beaucoup bath houses and cafes, and a hotel. Got to bed early—tired—and happy.

Sunday, August 11: I slept to the last minute this morning and still made breakfast. I knew there would not be anything to do and there wasn't. Nothing official to do, only write letters. I went up in the Officers' Club room (a low one story building with about six chairs, a table and a phonograph and no floor). There I wrote and listened to a heated argument, intermittently. The scrap was on the advisability or necessity of wearing roll collars when crossing the lines in airplanes. I think the affirmative won. After dinner I went to the beach and started walking in the longest direction. I had no aim in view or objective to reach, only an ambition to walk and about three hours. I figured out how I could bring down an average of five Germans a day excluding Sundays and then started home.

We had a fine entertainment in the evening. It started by the Chaplain getting up and telling a great line of stories and jokes. Then five girls gave an entertainment consisting of a lot of songs, dances, readings, etc. It was lots of fun. I doubt if the people in the States realize how much an entertainment like that means way off in a camp over here. I certainly am strong for the Y and what it is doing.

Letter, August 11. Dear Old Al: Since I wrote you last I've had a couple of classes and a good swim or two and have been to the grand town of Jean-de-Monts. The classes have all been more or less a review of what we had on gunnery at Issoudun. They have been made quite interesting though by the thought we may have to use some of the stuff we learn within the next month. Somehow or other that put a good deal of pep in the driest kind of a lecture.

The swims were wonderful; we have a long broad beach here all to ourselves. The water is warm and the air and breeze is warmer still. It is great to dive into the breakers and fight with the big swells and then come out on the hot sand to dry off. I don't think I like it quite as well as the swims at Lake George but it is pretty good considering that I am in the Army on active service in France. There aren't too many people who can spend two weeks on the sea shore. Tomorrow we start real work and I will be very glad of it. We have not had any flying yet and that always makes me sore. Well, that is all that has happened so far. I will write again soon. Lots of love, Percival

Letter, August 11. Dear Lucia: I went down to one of the towns yesterday evening to look it over. It was just like the sea-side towns over home. Little one-story lodges scattered around, a few grocery and butcher shops, numerous booths where they sold post cards and trinkets, and one or two pretty good hotels. The beach is lined with little cafes and bath-houses. The people, what there are of them, wander around in bare feet or wooden shoes half full of sand. The best-looking places and gardens are quite interesting until you see the house. They may be all right on the inside but the outside of the average Frenchman's house is pretty shabby-looking. I have thought a thousand times as I have traveled around this country, "These poor people don't know how to live, and don't know what life and comfort is." You never see pretty lawns, neat houses, clean grounds (especially about the stables), or shady trees. There is a saying that a Frenchman has no use for water except to put it under bridges. I guess that is about true.

Of course a great deal of this could be excused by the war. The people are tired out and sick of the thing—yet they have not the slightest thought of giving in an inch. They have given their sons, their money, their food, anything and everything that would be of use, and they will keep on giving—but they will never quit. We only meet and come in contact with the poor class. They are the ones who are feeling the war, but they never murmur. The richer ones can pay the prices and move around a little, but the others live their lives like their cows and hogs, in the same house with them.

I think I told you that we were very nicely situated in barracks, and that the food was very good. Those are two things you don't have to worry about when you are an Aviator. They have to give you good food and lodging or you won't be any good as a flyer. We are very fortunate in having a peach of a Commanding Officer and fine men all the way through the post offices. I started to swim home the other day, but about half way across I remembered I had a class, and had to come back. Love to all, Percival

Monday, August 12: We started work this morning, getting up at 5:00. It was the first day for the field so nothing was organized. After about an hour's sitting around they gave us each a fifteen minute ride in a Nieuport to get used to the country. There was a lot of trouble with the machines, mechanics, etc so we did not get anything done in the morning. I had a great swim when I came in. In the afternoon we did a little better. I got in 105 shots at the balloons. We each had a balloon about four feet in diameter. They were filled with hydrogen and strung up about a hundred [meters]. We would come in on them in a steep glide opening fire at about 200 yards and closing down at 100. They were mighty hard to hit as they bobbed around in the breeze so much and the planes bumped in the rough air. The balloons were up from the shore so that our shots hit the beach or the water. Each man had his own balloon and tried to shoot 200 shots but the guns jam most of the time. I don't know how many times I hit the mark but it came down all right.

Tuesday, August 13: Things went a little more smoothly today. We got up at five again and got to flying by seven. I got a ride in a Camel first of all. We ride in them to get used to them as we will have to shoot from that type of machine on the sleeve [a towed gunnery target]. I did figure eights and flew around very moderately. Later in the morning I got in 142 shots on the balloons. I brought it down early in the game and was shooting at it on the ground. Just as I stopped shooting on one round I saw two mechanics running for my balloon. I circled around close to see what they were going to do. They grabbed it and started to let out what gas was left. Then I started to dive again. Gee, the poor fellows. They did not dare run for fear I would shoot at the balloon before they got far enough away. So they rolled it up quick and sat on it trembling. I guess they thought I would see them and not shoot. Of course I had no intention of shooting. I got a pretty good score I think.

I had another ride in the Camel this afternoon and did some acrobatics at a good altitude. I did everything that machine would do—side-slips, vrilles, spirals, barrells, renversements, and loops, but I still don't like it as well as a Nieuport. I managed to get in 188 shots this afternoon. In the course of which I cleared two jams in the air. I also shot a hole through my propellor. I went to town along the beach to get my pictures but they weren't finished.

Letter, August 13. Dear Grace: I try to get a letter off every other day, but it is pretty hard to find anything to say that would be of interest to you all and not to the Huns, if they should be so fortunate as to capture one of my priceless masterpieces of Literary Art! Personally, I think they would have a job translating it—considering the writing and the spelling. I think they must be capturing all the mail from the States, as I have not had a letter from anywhere in about three weeks. That is always the way it is when you change stations over here. We fly in the early morning, swim, write letters, and eat, and fly again in the afternoon, and all this at a regular summer resort. I am losing my respect for "us Aviators"; we have it too easy. Love, Percival

Wednesday, August 14: Things did not go so well today. We only have four Nieuports and some of them are out of commission. I had a long ride on a Camel and managed to fly it on its back a little way. I also got a good tail slide. Business picked up a little in the afternoon. I learned how to calibrate ammunition and load belts. It is surprising how little ammunition is perfect, as it has to be for aviation at the front.

I got in another ride in the Camel. This time I learned how to run it on its back and hold it there till she quit running. I am going to swear off. The bug is getting me and I will kill myself if I don't quit. I will call off that stuff as I am too near my goal to get hurt. The mechanics are green here and you have to look the plane over minutely every time you go up. The balloons were pretty steady this afternoon and I got in 146 shots. During the shooting I cleared some crossfeeds and jams. The walk along the beach in the evening is wonderful and makes me sleep well.

Letter, August 14. Dear Old Al: My work is going finely. Though the school is new we get a very good course here and things are running quite smoothly. The swimming is still wonderful, especially on these hot days. Also it is great walking on the beach in the evening with a lovely cool breeze and the moon shining across the water as it does at Lake George. Lieutenant Morrison is in charge of training here. He was at Tours and knows you. He is a peach of a fellow and does everything possible for us. Well this is very short but I haven't much time. Love, Per

Gunnery School

Thursday, August 15: Most of the Nieuports were broken this morning and I had finished on the balloons anyhow so I took out my time on Camels. I managed to get in almost an hour. They are getting to feel better though I am not yet comfortable in them. They give me "good times in the air." I did not get up to shoot on the silhouettes in the morning. I had a little cold in my head so I did not go in swimming. As a result of the layoff I am about all right. We started in on the silhouettes this afternoon. They are easier to hit than the balloons but the air is very rough near them on account of the contour of the ground which makes shooting hard. I had great luck with my gun. She shot the full 200 rounds without a jam, stoppage, or misfire. I don't know what I got but it looked pretty good.

Friday, August 16: I had a bad day today. After breakfast I volunteered to go about eight miles down the beach and bring back a plane [a Camel] that Barton left down there the night before. The plane was in pretty good condition, though a couple of ribs were busted in each lower wing. I took off with it though and got out over the water about a hundred and fifty feet out and not over three feet up when a gust of wind hit me and one wing dipped; then the undercarriage hit and the next I knew I was sitting up to my neck in the water. It did not take long to get off my goggles and helmet and unfasten my belt. Then I climbed out on the trailing edge of the center plane and looked around. The plane was standing right on her nose and slowly sinking. The wings were both smashed off and little pieces of prop, struts, and spars were floating around on the water [Fig. 14]. I did not fall far but I was going about a hundred miles per hour. There were no boats around so I put my stuff in my pockets and swam ashore. My clothes and everything in them were about ruined. Besides my garments I had two pocket books, a note book, two watches, a fountain pen, a leather coat and helmet, gloves and goggles, a camera, and my new altimeter. The coat and stuff may come out all right, and a fellow cleaned my watch, but my camera and altimeter are ruined. I took them both apart, but they were already badly rusted. I may be able to get them fixed in Paris. I did not fly again that morning but this

Fig. 14. Percival Gates' wrecked Camel on the beach near St. Jean-de-Monts, France (OHTM)

afternoon I got in 200 shots on the silhouettes. I have got about the best score so far.

Saturday, August 17: I was a little stiff from my early swim yesterday but otherwise none the worse for wear. We went out on the field this morning but as there was only one ship in commission and that busted we came in early. I spent the entire morning trying to put the shutters of my camera together. It was worse than any watch I ever saw. I finally got it fixed though but I cannot get the proper adjustment.

After lunch I wrote letters and slept until four. We had a couple of ships when we got out there so we all finished up our 600 shots on the silhouettes. They were not very hard to hit and for the first 400 shots I got a pretty good percentage—58% for the first 200 and 88% for the second 200. 25% is good so you see I had pretty good luck. They also told me my shots were well-grouped. I just hope I can group some on a Boche plane when I get to the front. I stayed at home like a good boy this evening and wrote letters, home, to Alice, and to Russell. I did not mention my fall to anyone but Russell for fear of worrying the others.

Letter, August 17. Dear Father: The last few days have been pretty busy ones, so I've not been able to do as much letter writing as usual. I am still at St. Jean-de-Monts though I will not be here long enough for you to use that as an address. This course in gunnery is not long, and we get in a lot [of flying] during each day. I will finish before the end of next week if the weather stays clear and the planes stay in good condition. One could not ask for more beautiful weather and that, along with wonderful surf bathing, keeps one in the finest kind of shape. The food is also very good here, so you see I am having a regular rest up before my real work begins. From here I will be sent to an assignment station where I will wait assignment to some squadron at the front. However there is a pretty long intermission at that station I understand, so there is no use worrying for awhile, as it will be a month at least.

My work has been going pretty well. So far I have as high a score as anyone here. That does not mean much, but it is encouraging, at least. Our hours are quite long, but we don't do much in them. We start at 6:00 AM and stop at 10; then start again at 4 PM and stop at 8. The meals are 5:30, 12:00 and 8:15 so you can imagine the appetite worked up between times. By the way things are going, we will have the Germans licked by next spring I believe and we will all be home for a big summer vacation before taking the trip over here. We get a chance to travel around so much and see and live in so many different towns that a trip by car will be perfectly wonderful. I have got about half of it mapped out already. I think I will have to come home for a little while though, first. Then we can appreciate it more than ever.

We had a little excitement the other day. Some big guns to the north of us and apparently out to sea opened up full force and fired for about an hour. We had visions of the German navy coming down the coast, or the submarines attacking in force, but it only proved to be a little practice shooting up the coast. Oh this is a great life; carefree, happy, and exciting (at times). I don't think I ever will be able to settle down to the hum drum life of an office or farm or anything like that. You will have to figure out something more lively. I warn you I am getting the "Call of the Wild" and the "Wanderlust." Perhaps after I have been to the front for awhile I will get rid of some of my excess energy. Now I have got you all excited and you are saying "That boy is getting reckless." There is where you guessed wrong. My continuous holding in and carefulness is the cause of my high tide of spirits, and believe me that tide ebbs and flows very consciously.

Well I guess I have covered most of the news here, and as there is a concert about to take place in the adjoining room of this Y, I had better stop. Lots of love to every one of you dear honeys and don't you worry a minute. Percival

Sunday, August 18: I did not get up until 11:30, just in time for dinner. After dinner I wrote letters for a couple of hours and then took a walk down the beach. It is lots of fun for me to get off by myself on the beach or someplace and just sort of dream about anything and everything. I don't get homesick but I do love to dream about home and the times I have had. That all means a lot to us over here. Thank goodness no time, no distance, no war can take away the happy thoughts of the past. We had a mighty slim supper but I filled out at the Y. Then I wrote some more letters making six in all. That is another pasttime I get a lot of pleasure out of. It does not make a lot of difference who the person [is] so long as I know them well and think they will be interested in what is going on over here. I am pretty tired and will go to bed early.

Monday, August 19: We all got up late this morning so that by the time we got on the field the sleeve had been up a half an hour. Three fellows got up to shoot on it but one of them shot it off so they had to come down. Then they tried ten more sleeves but none of them opened. Finally they gave up in disgust. A sleeve is a long tube-shaped cloth affair that is towed behind another plane. It opens up by the wind and forms a sleeve-shaped tube about 10 feet long and three feet in diameter. The idea is to pull up along side of the towing ship, turn in sharply, shoot at the sleeve, and virage off it. In this way you get fine practice for deflection.

By noon I had a hard headache from my sinus tubes, or whatever they are, being stopped up. I went over to the hospital and got fixed up pretty well. In the afternoon I finally got up and shot on the sleeve. It was pretty hard to hit the thing but the four of us who shot on it got an average of 8%. McCoy came in late with a target ship and I never saw a fellow come closer to smashing up—twice he had the machine on the ground and both times he gave it the gun and just zoomed over the trees. He only missed getting killed by feet. There was nothing going on in the evening so I got to bed early.

Letter, August 19. Dear Old Al: There is a concert going on in the next room, and I am so full of dinner that I can hardly bend over. We have got the most wonderful chaplain here you ever saw. He is an old peach. The concert was a little late tonight so he got up and pulled off a line of stunts and jokes that almost drove the crowd into hysterics. I believe they'd rather have him up there than the regular show.

My work has been going pretty well. I am a little over half

through now, and so far I have as good a score as anybody here. I am really getting to think that I could really hit a Hun if he would stand still a minute. I at least have the satisfaction of knowing that I am as well trained as anyone who goes to the front. I will finish here the middle of next week and then I will see you again if you are still at Tours and have not started on your leave yet. I will go to O[rly] when I finish and ferry [aircraft] until I get assigned. It will probably be a month.

I will probably get down to Limoges and stop a while at Issoudun if Russ is still there, as he probably will be. I guess you had better address me after this as 2nd Lt, U. S. Air Service, Aviation Section, Unassigned, American Expeditionary Forces. That will reach me anywhere. Your loving brother, Percival

Tuesday, August 20: We got up on time this morning since we had been caught the morning before. I did not get to shoot in the forenoon however. My headache is all cleared up but I did not go in swimming for fear of getting more trouble. In the afternoon Hays and I got to shoot on a sleeve together. We were the only ones shooting and we got 11%. That is considered very good since 20% is perfect shooting allowing the other 80% for the cone of fire and the shaking of the gun.

Linderburg was towing the sleeve and as the next one was being shot at he started to come in. We guessed that he had engine trouble. He flew over the field on a glide and dropped the sleeve. Then as he turned to make a tour-de-piste his engine began to miss badly. Just as he got over our heads the thing quit. Lindy turned sharp to try for the field. He did not have room to dive for speed. The big machine dropped on one wing and started vrilling [spinning]. I don't know when I have watched a more horrible sight. Fortunately the plane was only a hundred feet up, and as it came down one wing hit the top of a cloth hangar. It smashed through, crashing on the other wing. We were only a hundred yards away so we got to the accident immediately. The fellow was thrown out of the back seat and not badly hurt. Lindy had a bad cut on his lip but was otherwise all right. A fellow in the hangar was struck by some of the beams and had his shoulder and arm badly broken. The whole affair was rather fortunate not to be more serious.

Letter, 20 August.   Dearest Mother: This morning we got up at 5:15 as usual but as there is quite a fog we will not be able to fly for a couple of hours. I have had my breakfast, made my bed, and adopted a little black kitten as a mascot for our section, and it isn't seven o'clock yet. The sun is out now so it will not be long before the flying will start. I like the work here better than any place I have been yet. It seems to be more practical. I still have a pretty good record for shooting. Your loving son, Percival

Wednesday, August 21:   We were promised that we would not have to get up early this morning but by hook or by crook they got a machine running and called us out at about 7:00. I sat on the field all the morning but did not get up. We quit early as the AR [Avion Renault—the tow ship] busted. At 10:00 we had a lecture by Lieutenant Steve Brodie* who had just returned from seven weeks flying with a French chasse squadron. He gave us some mighty good dope on how to equip ourselves for the front, what to expect while there, and some of his personal experiences. It was a mighty interesting talk. One thing was especially interesting. He said that during last month they made 104% replacements in the flyers. He said that a man was very lucky to live three weeks up there. I don't know how true his statements were but I am just as keen to get to the front as I was before. The doughboy lieutenants get theirs and I will take my chances on getting mine. We had some flying in the afternoon but I shot the sleeve off on my first burst so that ended it. I wrote some letters but I was not tired enough to get to sleep.

Letter, August 21.   Dear Old Al: I am afraid now that you will have left Tours before I get a chance to get over to see you. Then if Russ should finish up at Issoudun I would be entirely out of luck. Russ seems to be coming along all right although he is in a considerable of a hole. He doesn't know whether to hurry up for me or wait for Sam. He has given me orders not to go near the front till he has cleared the sky of the Huns. Poor old fellow, he is worried to death about me and I am about as worried about him. Then you, I suppose, worry about both of us. There really isn't any news here except that I am well and happy. Lots of love, Percival

Thursday, August 22:   I am so far behind in this diary that I will just outline the days briefly. I got in my flying in the afternoon after sitting around all the morning. I shot last on the individual sleeve and managed to get 35 hits giving me 15% which is the record for this school so far. There was no entertainment at the Y so I went for a walk. Otherwise I can never get to sleep.

Friday, August 23:   It was cloudy this morning so we did not get to fly. They said we would get it in the afternoon but by that time the AR target ship was busted so we did not get in anything. Lt. Morrison, the officer in charge of training, called me in and offered me the job of machine gun instructor. He said he gave me the chance because of my good work. He said I could get in good time in the air and shooting and that the position was only for three or four weeks. It was a soft job with some advantages and temptations but I could not bring myself to take it. First I did not want to stay around St. Jean any more. Second I was due for the front and was just crazy to go. I must get in on the big drive. So I turned down the job.

Letter, 23 August.   Dear Auntie: I am having a great old time. I have finished this school with the best record in shooting of any one of the ten in my class. We are the first ones through, so I cannot make a broader comparison. However, I have the satisfaction of knowing that I have stood first or second in each field or class I have been in since I came over. I say this not to boast but to assure you that I go to the front as well trained and as good a flyer as any of the new men. If I am sent soon I am ready. I know I can make myself obey instructions to the last detail and that is the most important thing, they tell me. Most fellows get into trouble through disobedience of orders. So you need not worry about me in that line.

I am to leave here tomorrow for my assignment station. On my way I expect to stop in to see Alice at Tours and then go to see Russ at Issoudun. My stay here has been very pleasant and just about long enough. I have got the "moving habit" so I don't care to stay in one place too long. Not that I have anything to say about it, but I am just contented to let the Army move me around. That is a rather fortunate trait. By the looks of things and the news we get in the papers, we are to have a drive pretty soon. I hope so, and I hope I am there to see it and help out. They say that the greatest stimulus that our boys ever get is the sight of an American plane flying over them. Well honey, save up lots of good things, for we will be home as soon as we get these Huns licked. Love, Percival

Saturday, August 24: We had some flying this morning and finished for good. We had orders to pack and get clearance which I fixed up in the morning. In the afternoon I went over to see poor old Linderburg who was feeling pretty low. At about 3 we got our orders and after some delay we got started for Challans. Brubaker*, Hays*, Lee*, Bartron* and myself were all that were left of the "big ten" of St. Jean [Fig. 15]. We got the 5:00 train to Nantes where we arrived at 9:30. I stayed at the station looking up possible connections till most train time. At 10:00 PM I was on my way to Tours. I had to stand most of the time but finally we got to Tours at 3:00 AM.

Sunday, August 25: At 3:35 I went to the Y Hotel but there were no rooms. I looked in all the other hotels but no "chambre." "Ce sont tout complait." I went back to the Y in disgust and managed to get two little wooden benches to sleep on. After an hour some majors and captains came in and I gave them one of my benches. We all sat up and waited for morning. At last it grew light. I went for a walk to get up an appetite and try to find out if Alice was at camp or on pass. No news so I took a chance after breakfast and walked out. Al was there all right but that was not all. Russ and Sam came in on their bicycles. We had a regular reunion all together but for some reason it fell through as far as I was concerned. First, I was on my way to the front. Second, Russ insisted that he was

Fig. 15. Gunnery school graduating class, St. Jean-de-Monts. From left: Henry Brubaker, Percival Gates, Harold Barton, J. Carroll Cone, Sterling Tompkins, Donald Hughes, John Lee, Frank Hays. (OHTM)

going to be killed very soon. He gets sick flying and won't tell anyone about it. Third, after Russ was gone Al told me that she was practically engaged to a fellow and was going to marry him when she got home. He seems to be a fine fellow but I don't know him at all. I left at 4:00 feeling pretty low. I took the 4:30 for Vierzon. From there I took the 10:30 for Limoges arriving at 3:00 AM.

PART 5

Ferry Pilot, Orly Field, Paris, France, 26 August to 7 September 1918

[After visiting his old friend, Bernadine Fennelly, at Limoges, Gates traveled to Paris for the next phase of his flying experience, ferry pilot at Orly Field. His name was added to the pilot pool, those pilots available for assignment to a combat unit, and he was temporarily tasked to ferry new and repaired aircraft from the supply center at Orly Field, on the southern edge of Paris, to training and combat units in various locations across France. He ferried aircraft from 28 August through 6 September, flying eight ferry missions in Camels and two in aircraft he had not previously flown, the Breguet 14 and the SPAD 13. His travels brought him into contact with a number of units and operating locations he had not previously seen, and he received valuable experience flying cross-country missions to a number of airfields near the front, including Colombey-les-Belles, the field to which he eventually reported for his combat assignment. Although Gates' tenure as a ferry pilot was brief, his ferry flights took him to new fields and terrain. He was able to visit his sister at Tours and visit friends at St. Jean. He traveled across much of northern France by airplane and train, and experienced his first night bombardment while waiting for the train at Toul.

While flying as a ferry pilot, he displayed evidence of the increasing strain of flying as he cracked up a Camel he was flying while landing at Orly. But his spirit and attitude remained positive; offered a non-combat flying position by some friends at Paris, Gates turned it down and awaited word of an assignment to a combat unit. When he completed this final phase of his pre-combat preparation, Gates had accumulated a total of 110 hours of flying time. This amount of flying time was not fully adequate for one about to enter a combat unit, but it was nearly triple the hours of flying time with which pilots of the Royal Air Force had been reporting to their combat units two years earlier. More importantly, Gates felt mentally ready to participate in the war.]

Monday, August 26: At 3:30 I was in bed in the little Red Cross Rest Room next to the station. I woke up at 9:00, got dressed and breakfast and went up to Base Hospital 13 to look up Bernadine. She had been on night duty and though I tried to dissuade her she got up and came out to walk. We took dinner at the Central Hotel and went out in the country to bike for a couple of hours. Bernadine is only a friend and a pal, nothing more. She was feeling low and so was I so we had a mutual condolence party. We got back home by six, so that she could get supper and go on duty again. She is a peach and has been like an older sister to me. After supper I got another bunk at the Red Cross and went to sleep at eight thirty.

Tuesday, 27 August: The MP woke me at 1:45 AM in time to catch the 2:16 for Paris after a bite to eat. I sat with a doughboy second lieutenant who was on his way to the U. S. He told me a lot of interesting things about the front. The train was very crowded so we had to take seats 3rd class. He changed at Vierzon and I got standing room in a 1st class [coach] at Orleans. I stood to Paris where I arrived about 10:00. I went to the Richmond Y Hotel in a Red Cross bus but only left my stuff there and took dinner. I walked around Paris a few hours and took the 2:00 truck for Orly.

Got out here, reported, drew equipment, put in for a ship in the morning, and started writing up my diary. I did not get any ship [to ferry] so I spent the day looking over the ships here.

Tuesday, August 27: I tried for another ship this morning but there was nothing doing. About ten o'clock an orderly came in and told me that the sergeant major wanted to see me. I went up expecting orders but nothing doing. I was sent in to the Captain who accused me of delaying a day and a half in Paris on my way from St. Jean. He said they needed pilots so bad they would have to take disciplinary action. He confined me to the post for ten days. Then he wanted to put me on the ground but I kicked and showed him how inconsistent he was. The other four of my bunch got ordered out but I did not get mine. That makes me kind of sore but if I get out soon I will be all right.

Wednesday, August 28: I hung around the barracks all this morning writing letters and waiting for orders. About 10:30 I played some tennis with Riddick and had some good exercise. In the afternoon I got orders to go over to Le Bourget to bring back a Sopwith Camel. Four of us rode over in a car to the field which belonged to the English. The old Camel had a "monosoupape" [engine] in it which was new to me. However, when they got her started she ran like a house afire. You sure had to hold her nose down. I got her down at the field and managed to get in safely. The other three were out of luck. One caught on fire as he got on the field. Another ran into a building, and the third did not even get her [started].

Letter, August 28. Dear Frederick: I have been moving around for the last four or five days, so my letter writing has been sadly neglected. I finished at St. Jean last week and started for *here*. On my way I stopped at Tours. Alice was there looking finely and in good spirits [Fig. 16]. Fortunately while I was there Russ and Sam walked in. Wasn't that luck! We had a great reunion just like the one we had when I first got here. I stayed to dinner with Alice and took the afternoon train out. I had a very short stop at Paris

Fig. 16. Percival and Alice Gates, Tours, France (OHTM)

yesterday, but I did not have time to see much. It is certainly a beautiful city. It is lots of fun to hunt up the places I have seen so often in pictures, and see the originals. The only thing is, it would take about three weeks to see all I would like to.

The chances are I won't be here more than a few days, though. I am in the "zone of advance" now, so I cannot tell you the names of any more places I may be at. Well, my opinion, for what I have read in the papers, is that there is to be a big scrap pretty soon and that it will be the turning point of the war. We will smash the lines and show the Germans that they are licked before winter. By spring we will have so many men over here that there will be nothing to it. If the Huns realize that, they will probably try for peace terms this winter. See how close that turns out to be true. I hope to get in in time for the drive, and I think I will. Well this is just a short note but it is enough to show you that I am well and happy. Love to all, Percival

Letter, August 29: Dear Al: I got down to Limoges all right and had a fine time down there for half a day. Bernadine has been a fine friend to me. We were together most of the time on the boat and while we were at Brest we saw the country together. We know each other pretty well, but as far as anything serious goes we are just pals. I did not get to see much of Paris on my way here as I was already late in reporting and did not want to delay. This is a great place for flying different kinds of ships, but I hope to get ordered out soon. I must get up there for the big fun whether I get through it or not.

I saw just enough of Paris to want to see more but I don't think I will have much of a chance. Yesterday the Captain called me in and confined me to the post for 10 days for being 36 hours late in reporting. That does not bother me much though as I can still ferry until I get my orders. How did Russ come out on his air work? I think he will have sense enough to change to something else if he finds that he really isn't built for chasse. Give my best to Woody if you see him. He is at Tours, I believe. I am giving your name "to notify in case of emergency"—you can notify home probably quicker than the Army. Well I must stop now and look for orders. Lots of love, Percival

Thursday, August 29: I made out a report for my ship and put in for another. This time they had plenty of ships and by noon they had my orders ready. I took a Spad to Colombey-les-Belles. It was a great trip. I had never run a Spad before so I had plenty to do watching the gauges and trying to keep on course. I got to Venetz all right where I stopped for gas and oil. From there on I just went by the sun till I got to Gondrecourt. It was a beautiful trip from there on especially through the hills. I got to Colombey at about six, had dinner, and took the truck for Toul at 7:30. The train for Paris left at 9:00 which we caught after a cup of hot chocolate and doughnut at the Officers' Y.

Friday, August 30: The train pulled into Paris at 8:00 and we got the 9:00 truck for Orly. After making a report, I got a hot bath and dinner. At the noon roll call I got assigned to ride as passenger to Venetz and take a Spad from there to Colombey. I did not enjoy my ride much as I think I could have run the plane better than my pilot. When I arrived I found that my ship was not ready and would not be ready today. I got a good meal and a room in the hospital as that was the only bed on the post.

Saturday, 31 August: I got up this morning very much rested out and after a wash in hot water and a good breakfast I was ready for my trip. My ship was ready at 10 and I started off. It was a very dark day, low clouds and frequent storms. It was lots of sport to fly along dodging the rain and trying to keep on course. Everything went well for a while until I got lost. I came to a town which I thought to be Toul. After looking around for half an hour to find Colombey I gave it up and landed at a French aerodrome. There I discovered I was at St. Dizier. From there on it was easy going. I got to Colombey in time for dinner and took the noon truck in to Toul. I spent the afternoon and evening in town looking it over. It was a very interesting old town with a high wall and moat around it. There were hundreds of officers and men there all *busy*. After a good dinner at the Hotel Metz I took the train back.

Sunday, September 1: Had a big day today. I got to Orly at 10:00 and immediately got a ship for Venetz. By 11:00 I was in the air. The clouds were very low so I had some more fun. I got down to the 5th Air Depot in time for dinner and left my ship there. At 1:00 we took a truck to Troyes where our train was to come in. We had a funny time with an old Belgian who was about half crazy and wanted to buy us all drinks. We got the 4:02 out which arrived in Paris at about 8:00. I took dinner at the University Union and got a room at a hotel.

Monday, September 2: I had a great old sleep last night and came out very much rested. There were no more ships in the morning so I took dinner with Alex and June. They were working on experiments which were quite interesting. I just got a hint from Alex that he had turned my name in to be transferred to his department as a permanent pilot. He was mighty kind to try to keep me from going to the front and thus prolong my chances but somehow I cannot see that system. I am ready to go and I must go. I nipped the thing in the bud and got out of it.

In the afternoon I got a ship for Venetz. Though I hurried things up I could not get off until 3:00 and that got me in too late for the afternoon train. Shook and I got the evening one out though which had a diner on it, so we rode in style. I came on out to camp for the night and got here at 1:30. It was late and I was tired so you can imagine how I felt to find some one else in my bed. I got in somebody else's though so it was all right.

Tuesday, September 3: There was quite a bunch of us this morning but I was lucky enough to get a plane to ferry. It was a Breguet. I had never flown any large plane before but I got a sergeant to tell me what the different buttons, levers, and switches were. It was a wonderful old plane to fly, just like riding in a pullman. When I got to St. Dizier my engine began to miss. I did everything I could think of but she still backfired. I landed on the French field there.

They told me my radiator shutter was broken but they could not fix my backfiring. I waited about an hour for my motor to cool off and went up again. She still kicked so I figured that the mixture was too lean and if I used my choke (for starting only) I could fix my trouble. It worked fine and I landed at Colombey successfully.

I walked and rode to Toul right away and spent the afternoon there. After quite a pleasant stay I got the 9:00 train out. As I was standing in the station the whistles and sirens blew and the search lights began to play around in the sky. We could distinctly hear the low buzz of a Hun plane. Then a big search light signaled dot dot dash, dot dot dash, dot dot dash and went out. We watched for the password from the plane but it did not come. The lights flared up in the sky and the batteries on all sides opened up with a roar. The sky was filled with little flashes and bangs. It was a great sight. Three planes passed over us but they were bound for further back. The train pulled in as usual and I was lucky enough to get a seat and some sleep.

Letter, September 3. Dear Family: As you know, I finished up at my last school and came to O[rly] to await orders to the front. Well, they have not come through yet, so I am putting in my time ferrying ships from one place to another. It is wonderful sport though it is very hard work. For instance, I took a ship at 11:30 this morning from O[rly]. It was a type I had never flown before. After about 1 hour and 10 minutes flying, the engine got hot and I had to land in a French field to let it cool off. Then I went on and arrived at my destination half an hour later. It was a beautiful 200 mile trip over wonderful country. The ship flew finely except for my little overheating, and the weather was clear. There is nothing to compare to "seeing France from an Airplane." I got in to [Toul] at 3:00 PM.

[I am writing in] an Officers' Club YMCA fixed up very comfortably with a peach of an old lady in charge. She has just served hot chocolate, crackers, doughnuts, and two pieces of fudge for afternoon tea. There is a small canteen attached where you can buy some crackers for the trip home tonight. I will get dinner here and take the train for Paris at 9:10 this evening. There is no sleeping car and I will be very lucky to get even a seat. Last time I came through I could not get a seat so I put on my "Teddy Bear" [flying suit] and lay down in the aisle and slept.

I will get to Paris at about 7:00 AM tomorrow, report to O[rly] at 9:00, and will probably be flying another ship somewhere by 10:00. That is the way things go with me. I get an awfully good sleep about every other night. Oh but I am having a great time, though! First I see the country from the air, and then I see it from the train. On the side I am learning to run about every plane made, and my mileage vouchers cover all expenses about three times over. I don't know how long this will last, but when I get my orders I will be on a job even more enjoyable than this.

I saw June Roberts and Alex Stevenson the other day and took dinner with them. They are permanently stationed at O[rly]. I hope to get a ship to Issoudun or Tours tomorrow. That would be lots of fun to drop in on Alice or Russell. Well, I did not get in my "Monthly Report" but I am in fine health and I think you can see that my spirits are pretty high. I hope to get to the front before the drive that seems to be going on is over. I feel that I am ready and when my time comes I will be mighty glad to go in. Lots of love, Percival

Wednesday, September 4: I got out this morning in good time but there was no chance for a plane. I sat around all day and finally at 4:00 they sent me off in a side car to get a Camel which had panned [force-landed] at Juvisy. I thanked the French C.O. of that field and took the plane. In landing at Orly I came in with the wind, chevalled, busted both tires, scraped a wing, and broke the tail skid. I was just too worn out to know what I was doing and it was a signal for me to lay off and get some sleep. I saw a peach of a show at the Y in the evening. Miss Somebody Franklin and company. It cheered me up quite a lot.

Thursday, September 5: I got a fine sleep last night and was feeling fine this morning. When I got to the office they had a plane ready for me. It was a Camel for St. Jean-de-Monts by way of Tours. Nothing could have suited me better. As soon as the weather cleared a little I started off. The trip to Tours was rather uninteresting except for the fact that my motor was pooping all the way. I got there in good time to take dinner with good old Woody. He is chef-de-piste of the observers' field. I had my plane fixed up and spent four hours with Alice. We had a fine visit and I had a chance to get to know her friend Ray better. He is a peach of a fellow. I started off at 4:00 and tried to do some stunts but sadly failed as the old Camel would not do anything.

I followed the river down passing through several storms and praying that my motor would get me to St. Jean. I got there all right and met the old boys on the field. I went to mess and saw good old Chaplain Griffiths. MacRoy and Linderburg were in their room after dinner and I had a visit with them. We all went to the Y after a while and had some lemonade and cookies. Then the chaplain took me down to town to a dinner party which we found to be all over but the drinking. Though we did not drink we had a good time. Got home late and slept soundly.

Friday, September 6: I missed my 6:45 truck this morning but by the aid of a side car I caught up with it. Then followed a three hour ride in a slow truck. We got to Nantes at about 10:30 and had an hour to kill before train time. There I managed to get five copies of the *Fly Paper* with the picture of the graduating class. The train was a little late but as there were plenty of seats I did not mind that much. I met a young lady on the way in to dinner and had quite an interesting time trying to talk to her. She seemed to be quite nice. Got to Paris about 9:00 and made for a room and bath—both of which I got, with a good sleep added on.

Saturday, September 7: I got in to Orly early this morning and found that my orders were being made out for Colombey-les-Belles. I packed up my stuff and got my clearance by three o'clock. Got my orders and cleared out of Orly. We all had a time with our baggage at the station. There were about 90 of us all trying to check our stuff at once. I got through about 6:00. Johnson, David, Benson, and I took dinner at the University Union and then beat it for our train. Luckily we all got seats but not much sleep.

PART 6

Assignment to the 185th Aero Squadron, Colombey-les-Belles, France, 8 to 29 September 1918

[On the 7th of September, Gates received orders to report to the 1st Pursuit Group at Colombey-les-Belles for further assignment to one of the Group's units. The 1st Pursuit Group was comprised of four of the most famous American combat squadrons at the front, the 94th Aero Squadron, the 95th Aero Squadron, the 27th Aero Squadron, and the 147th Aero Squadron. The best known figure in the 94th was Eddie Rickenbaker, America's leading ace; the 95th was the squadron in which Quentin Roosevelt, son of President Theodore Roosevelt, had met his death in aerial combat; and the 27th featured Frank Luke, who was earning fame as a "balloon buster." In addition to these well-known units, the 1st Pursuit Group was establishing a new squadron, the 185th Aero Squadron, originally intended as a day pursuit squadron like the other four. On the 8th of September Gates and a number of his friends signed on with the 185th; they were enthused about reaching the front and were pleased to be associated with 1st Pursuit Group veterans.

Because the unit was in the process of filling out its personnel roster and acquiring aircraft and maintenance equipment, flying activity initially consisted of ferrying, training, and orientation flights. From the 15th to the 29th of September, Gates flew training and ferry flights in SPAD 7 and SPAD 13 aircraft. This was his first experience in a SPAD 7, although he had flown the more challenging SPAD 13 when he was acting as a ferry pilot at Orly. According to his logbook, he also flew the Salmson, a two-place observation aircraft. Although he was excited about his association with the 1st Pursuit Group, his enthusiasm was dampened both by the rainy weather from the 8th through the 22nd, and by the lack of combat activities. Still, Gates kept his spirits up, for he sensed that he would eventually see combat.]

***

Sunday, September 8: We arrived in Toul at about eight o'clock and went right to the Officers' Y. There we got a good breakfast [and] left our baggage while we made a tour of the town. After about two hours we met and went out to the road to catch a truck for Colombey. Fortunately we got a limousine out. After signing in and getting a bunk, Johnson and David went downtown and got signed up in the 185th Aero Squadron. Johnson came back and told Philip Benson* and me about it so we got signed up too. We collected our stuff and went right over to the squadron. The camp was about two kilometers from Colombey set back in a woods. The barracks are very comfortable with rooms for three and a stove in each room. We have an orderly whom we call Kerensky. The mess is fine and the Commanding Officer (Lt. Lowe*) is a peach. About eight o'clock we got a truck and went down after our baggage. After a long search we got three out of four of our bedding rolls. The [French workers] were wild because we had no checks but after putting the stuff in the truck and giving the men some cigarettes they cooled off a little. On the way home we ran into a motorcycle and side car. Fortunately no one was hurt.

Monday, September 9: It was rainy this morning so we could not get some planes we were scheduled to get. Most of us went to the other camp to get the rest of our baggage, sign out, and get our written orders. The rest of the bunch that was at Orly came in during the morning and our squadron was filled up. I sat around and wrote letters all the afternoon. We had another fine mess and went to bed early.

Letter, September 9. Dear Franklin: Since September 2nd I've been on the jump all the time. My last ferry trip was down to my old gunnery school. On my way I stopped in for four hours to see Alice. She was just as happy and well as ever. When I got back I found that my orders were waiting [for] me for the distributing station near here. I arrived after a very hurried trip yesterday morning. Inside of a few hours I was assigned to this squadron permanently. I am now a full fledged member of the 185th Aero Squadron. We are pretty well back of the lines and will get some practice before we move up. We have a fine personnel of enlisted men and post [administrative] officers. The flyers are a great bunch. I have known most of them from ground school [Georgia Tech] and Park Field. I would say I am pretty lucky. My light is going out, so I must stop. Love to all, Percival

Tuesday, September 10: It was still raining this morning so I got permission to go to Nancy in a *car*. It was a beautiful ride through the mountains and valleys from Toul to Nancy. The Doc was with us (Doc Cabot). He was an old peach and lots of fun. I got badly stung on the whole at that town. First of all I bought a pair of boots at the rate of 220 francs. It is a mighty fine pair of boots though. Next I got a pair of britches. They were also very fine but they cost 130 francs. After buying a flashlight and a few other things I went about broke. After spending most of my money I started to look over the town. It was pretty well busted up around the [train] station. The Huns have worked hard to blow up that station. On the way home we ran out of gas and just got home on some that we borrowed from a French ambulance. There was a good deal of shooting up over the line this evening. I wish I could get over to help out.

Letter, September 10. Dear Alice: You will have to pardon the awful exhibition of flying I gave you as I left, as it was absolutely impossible for me to make that miserable Camel do anything. She would not even barrell [roll]. I will come down to see you again when I get my own little s[hip]. Thank you very much for the towels and chewing gum, it was sweet of you to be so thoughtful of me honey. I got to St. J[ean] all right and saw all my old pals there. That Chaplain's name is Griffiths. G. A. I think. He is an old peach and was as cordial to me as if he had known me for ten years.

I have been assigned to the 185th Aero Squadron which is stationed just back of [Colombey]. Please write Russ and the family so they can know. We are being organized and will not get into the mix-up for a little while yet. We have fine enlisted personnel and fine ground officers. The flyers are mostly fellows I have known for months at ground school, Camp Dick, and Issoudun. We have a peach of a C.O., too, which helps a lot.

We are very comfortable here with good quarters and a fine mess. However, as soon as soon as we get organized and equipped we will move into our real position and take up operations. It is great to hear the old guns booming at the front and see the flashes and flares at night. I must stop now and write up my diary. Lots of love, Percival

Wednesday, 11 September: It was a little clearer this morning so we went over to get some planes. Then it started to rain. I stayed in the barracks and took lunch up there but still it rained. At last it looked better and I went down to the hangar again. The minute I got there it started to rain again. I quit at last and went to the armament officer to get a couple of hours' instruction on the Marlin [machine gun]. It is still raining this evening. The guns are booming heavily in the distance and it is mighty significant. We had a little party this evening, toast made over our stove and Quartermaster sardines.

Thursday, September 12: Raining again today though it looks as if it may clear. I went over to the First Air Depot to get my machine and finally succeeded in getting my plane back. In the evening I went up the road for a walk. The guns were booming off in the distance and as it grew dark I could see the flashes. It is good to be so close. I only wish I could get over the lines. They say they started the drive yesterday but we have not heard anything yet.

Friday, September 13: It is raining again this morning. Johnson and I did not get up till late, just in time for breakfast. As there was nothing going on we got permission to go to Toul for a day. We walked to Colombey in the pouring rain. There we caught a truck for Toul. There was not much to do in the town but we left some films at the store across from the Officers' Club and took dinner at the Metz Hotel. Then we went to call on a friend of Johnny's up at Base Hospital 45. Had a nice little visit there and went back to town. Johnny bought a rabbit and I bought a musk melon. We are due to have a little feast tonight. We got a touring car home so we made good time. All but two of the fellows got back from Moulin. Clark* smashed up somewhere and is in the hospital and Benson is lost. Johnnie is now cooking the rabbit so I will have to join him.

Letter, September 14. Dear Lucia: I told you in my last letter to Franklin that I have been assigned to the 185th Aero Squadron. We are very comfortably located. This is a fine place; far enough back of the lines to be pretty safe from bombing and yet close enough to hear the old guns roar all day and night. You read about the little push we made. It was a great sight in the night time. The flashes, flares, and booming were great; and then to think of what our boys were doing to the Huns! This morning while we were out on the field we saw our Archy open up on a Hun plane. Later I heard that he had been brought down. Very few of them get across our lines. We have got them where we want them. I don't think there will be a spring drive. However, I am alone, almost, in this wild idea. I think we will break the Boche spirit this fall.

It has been raining most of the time since I've been at this place. In fact this is the first day it has been clear. Yesterday another fellow and I went to a large town near by to do some shopping. It was a pouring rain, but that made no difference. We brought back two boxes of YMCA chocolates, a bag of grapes, one of plums, a musk melon, and a rabbit. We got the cook to salt and parboil the beast and in the evening we fried it over our little stove in our room. Some party, I tell you, with fried rabbit, sardine on toast, candy, musk melon, and Campbell's beef soup for any one who wished it. In the distance you could hear the guns boom and see the flashes through the rain. Inside we sat around our little stove and ate, told stories, and read the "Rhymes of a Red Cross Man." You could hardly think we were at the front. I am glad I am in Aviation, though I do feel that we have it pretty soft. It will be more worth while when we have better weather and get our full equipment. Are you getting all my letters? Lots of love, Percival

Letter, September 16. Dear Grace: When I was down at Tours about two weeks ago to see Alice, I heard that you might come over here to do some kind of work. I suppose you have already decided what you are going to do and you have probably put in your application, but in case you have not had much success I can suggest two other possibilities. You have tried the YMCA, of course, and for all I know you are in it; however, if you have not been successful, you might try a "nurse's aide." I believe you would need very little training and there is no doubt but there is a need for girls in that line. You would be with other girls, nurses, etc. so you would not be as lonesome as you might be off in a Y hut.

The only other thing is the Red Cross Canteen. That is a good deal like the Y, only you would be stationed at a railway center, transfer depot, or some place like that. The surroundings are not so nice but you would not have much personal contact with any one bunch of men as Alice has had. However, it is a great work. The poor fellows come into these stations about starved and it must be great to be able to give them something to eat and a place to sleep. As I say, though, the work is harder and rougher than the Y. I don't mean by that that you would receive any insults nor hear any swearing. That does not occur in our Ys or Red Cross rest huts. Father and Mother need not worry about that. An American girl who comes over here to do good service in a Y or other place is perfectly safe from harm or insult. I favor the Nurse's Aide idea more than anything else—though you would have to look it up carefully, as I don't know much about the duties etc. So much for that.

I am having a good time, as usual. This is a very nice little camp and a fine bunch of fellows. We have not got all our equipment yet, so we just fly around to get practice. Love to all, Percival

Letter, September 19. Dear Father: We've not been doing much since my last letter to Grace, as the weather has been so bad. The work has been pretty easy, and not as trying as I should have expected. Also the fine bunch of flyers and ground officers have made it mighty pleasant. It is very difficult to write much, as everything of interest is censorable. I have not had any very interesting personal experiences, as we are working back of the lines for a while to get broken in slowly. Here I am in my little 20x20 room in a nice dry barracks seated at a writing desk in a real chair. We have candles for light and a nice little stove to keep us warm. There are three other fellows in here with me who are peaches. As a result we get along finely. Well it is time for dinner so I must stop. Lots of love, Percival

Letter, September 22. Dear Mother: I've been having a pretty easy time lately, as it has been raining most of the time. We've been having some great hunting in the forests near by. So far we have not gotten anything but there is always a chance to get something big, like a wild boar, all of which makes it interesting. On clear days we do some flying, but not much, as yet. Yesterday I had a great day. I started off at 8:30 AM with twelve other fellows in two Cadillac touring cars. We took a 96 mile ride to a certain air depot, stopping on the way for dinner. From there we took planes to another place. The cars followed as best they could. We took dinner, or rather supper, at the other town and came back for a 60 mile ride by moonlight. That was a wonderful party. Night before last they had a show here in the Y—the Craig company gave "Baby Mine." It was crude, as far as scenery went, but the acting was fine. It was a great show all the way through. We can appreciate those things now. I must stop for bed. Love, Percival

Letter, September 27. Dear Alice: Sam came up the other day and is now stationed here with me. It is great to see him again. Of course he gave me all the latest dope on you and Russell but it was not the same as hearing from you direct. I am mighty glad Russ is in the work he is [Fig. 17]. I wish he could get away from Issoudun but I told you all before that he could not stand Field 8 work. I don't think he will ever get over his trouble.

Things are very quiet up here as far as our work is concerned. We are not in action yet but we are due to start pretty soon. I have been doing a good deal of flying of all kinds. It is a good time and place to get time in the air. We have our own little ships to play around in and our own mechanics to take care of it. A couple of times I have taken a 1918 Cadillac to another place about 96 miles away, and flew a ship from there to a depot and taken our car back. It is pretty nice riding around in cars after flying so long. This letter must be very disconnected as I am in the midst of a very talkative crowd so I hardly get a line at a time.

Just now they are discussing various kinds of drinks and their effects on the human body. I get a good deal of kidding about not drinking or smoking. It puts me in a rather embarrassing position at times. However I don't mind as it is all in good fun. We had a party last night; there were about 40 nurses over from one of the hospitals near by. I cannot say I had much of a time as there was too much champagne for the good of the party. I like my nurse friends a good deal better than the ones who were here. By the way, I got the most wonderful box of fudge from Bernadine you ever saw. I can't imagine where she got the stuff to make it. She is an old peach and has been a mighty good friend to me. Well I must stop now and try to get to bed. Lots of love, Percival

Letter, September 29. Dear Auntie: Your speaking of the care you take in saving money, gasoline, and food makes us ashamed over here. The way we use things is a crime. Of course it has to be done and that is why you have to save. I was just thinking of a trip I had the other day. It would have cost me a year's salary. First, the government has given me a fur-lined coat with a fur collar and waterproof, a fur-lined Teddy Bear, fur collar and waterproof, a plane helmet and fur-lined (one fur) gloves, two pairs of any kind of goggles I wish, and a light Teddy Bear. Also a pair of heavy

Fig. 17. Russell Gates and Moraine aircraft, Issoudun (OHTM)

fleece-lined boots to wear over our shoes. That is all a part of our equipment "at the front." Then on top of that, the old U. S. gave me a $10,000 plane for my exclusive use and work. We are not operating yet as the full quota has not arrived. Sam came up here the other day and is stationed in the same camp with me. He will be with me from now on I believe. It is too bad Russ could not come too, but he is best off where he is. Well, you old honeys, don't worry as I am having the time of my life. Lots of love, Percival

PART 7

Temporary Duty with the 27th Aero Squadron, Rembercourt, France, 30 September to 17 October 1918

[Gates' long-expressed wish to see action was unexpectedly fulfilled on the 30th of September, when he was suddenly transferred, along with two or three other pilots, from the 185th Aero Squadron to the 27th Aero Squadron, located at Rembercourt. The 27th had recently lost several pilots, including Lt. Frank Luke, who had failed to return from a mission on the 29th. In addition, the Meuse-Argonne offensive had just begun, and air support was essential for the advancing American infantry. Gates' good gunnery scores probably marked him as a likely replacement pilot. Gates received only two training flights (flown in one day) before he flew his first combat patrol over the lines. In the subsequent nine days (2–10 October) he flew eight combat missions.

The patrols with which he flew encountered enemy aircraft twice, and once he nearly lost his life when he was forced to crash-land in barbed wire in the front lines after his engine failed. His logbook shows that the patrol altitudes during this period never exceeded 2000 feet, indicating that the 27th Squadron was assigned to low-level sector patrol. Flying at low level made the patrols especially susceptible to attack from above, although the generally cloudy weather protected them from enemy attacks. During one of his patrols, however, a number of German aircraft dove down to attack. Fortunately, only one pilot was wounded, and he managed to return and land safely. Gates was quickly accepted into the 27th Aero Squadron, partly because he displayed a positive attitude, partly because he knew many of the pilots from previous training locations, and partly because many of them had trained at Tours and knew Gates' sister, Alice.

Gates' tenure with the 27th Aero Squadron was one of the highlights of his tour in France. The 27th featured such famed fliers as Joseph Wehner and Frank Luke, both of whom had been killed in action before Gates joined the squadron, and the pilots in the squadron had accounted for over fifty victories. Gates took his combat preparedness tasks seriously, reading the available literature, asking questions of the experienced pilots, resting himself well. He was an aggressive member of the squadron, never missing a patrol except when his aircraft malfunctioned. Although new in the squadron, he was not hesitant about taking over the lead of a mixed group of aircraft on his second patrol, and he spotted a flight of enemy aircraft before others in his group. These were not the usual characteristics of a novice combat pilot. Even his aversion to drinking stood him in good stead in the squadron; while the others participated in the almost nightly squadron parties, he wrote letters home and good naturedly accepted his comrades' teasing. On at least one occasion the squadron commander of the 27th Aero Squadron, Captain Alfred Grant, appointed Gates as acting commander and duty officer, probably because he knew he could count on Gates to keep a clear head in the midst of squadron celebrations.

By flying with the 27th, Gates was fulfilling the dream that had carried him safely through the hazards of training for the previous nine months. But it is also apparent that the sudden strain of combat activity was taking its toll; his last entry in his flight log was made on the 10th of October, on the day of his last flight with the 27th, and one day after he narrowly escaped serious injury in a crash-landing. One week later, he made his final entry in his diary, on his last day with the 27th Aero Squadron.]

Letter, September 30. Dear Father: Things have changed a good deal since my last letter. I have been transferred out of the 185th into the 27th Aero Squadron in the 1st Pursuit Group. Now I am at the front and right in the middle of a big scrap. I was transferred for replacement in the 27th and I consider myself pretty lucky. This is the best and most noted squadron in the group, and of course you know that the 1st Pursuit is the best on the front. The boys have been doing wonderful work and I am proud to be with them and have the opportunity to work with them. It is a great advantage to be with an old group and old flyers. Our flight leaders are old and experienced; they know when to attack and how to do it. Our mechanics are fine and of course our ships are OK. In fact, conditions are ideal for me. While I was with the 185th I got a lot of time on these machines, so it is not like taking up a new type.

Tomorrow I will have spent four months in France. I am a good deal better off than I was when I came I am sure. I never was feeling better or in better condition. I have been very careful about drinking water. For the past two months I have not had a drop of water that has not been strongly medicated or boiled. Usually all the liquid I get to drink is a cup of coffee at breakfast and a cup of tea or chocolate at supper. However I am certainly thriving on it and as yet I have not had to touch a drop of wine, beer, or any kind of liquor. I've not smoked a cigarette, pipe, cigar, or anything else and I have a clean record for conduct. In other words, my four months in France have not had the slightest ill effect on me mentally, physically, or morally. Thanks to my bringing up. Lots of love to you all, Percival

Letter, September 30. Dear Cousin Helen: I have moved again. The last squadron I was with was not fully equipped so we did not operate much. Now I am with a new one, or rather another old one. It is with the 1st Pursuit Group right up on the front. I am here as replacement and will start work right away. Last night I had my first experience with French billets. The billet was an old church divided into about a hundred little rooms just big enough to accommodate a bed, wash stand, and chair. It was funny when I woke up this morning to look up at a beautiful arched ceiling dotted with gold stars. I thought it was still night till I saw the sun trying to come in through some stained glass windows which were somewhat the worse for the spattering of a bomb that had fallen near by. Oh this is a great business.

I am writing this letter on a table captured from the same source [the Germans]. In the near distance I hear the old guns booming away in one solid roar. Just over that hill is one of the hottest fights yet, and tomorrow I hope to be in it. That will be exactly four months from the day I landed on French soil. My! it seems as though I have been here four years, and yet again it seems as if it was only a week since I was eating "the last supper" at the hotel in Fort Worth. Give my love to all the family and write when you have time. Love, Percival

Tuesday, October 1: I spent most of the morning reading over orders, writing letters, and studying the map and types of machines the Huns use. There is plenty of information to be had and lots to learn. It is a great advantage to be in this squadron. Although it is not the oldest it has the record for victories. Then of course the group is ahead of all others on the front. There are old men for flight leaders who know the game and they take care of us new ones.

In the afternoon I went with eight others to get ships from Bar-le-Duc [Fig. 18]. It is quite a ride down there by truck and it took some time to get the ships, so we did not get back until late. I was hoping to have one of the ships assigned to me but there weren't enough of them to go around. In the evening I talked at length with the old men and got as much dope as I could. It helps a lot to have such a source of information. There was a wild party in our tent but I did not take part.

Letter, October 1. Dear Old Al: I am now in the 27th Aero Squadron of the 1st Pursuit Group. It is the best squadron in the

Fig. 18. Map of front near Verdun

best group so I am pretty lucky. There is plenty of action here, so I hope to get started tomorrow. I am the only one in my flight who is green and new so there again I am lucky. It is great to be with this bunch that is the best in the flying corps. There is a fellow here in my flight named H. W. Nicholson* who wants to be most kindly remembered to you. He said to tell you that he will take good care of me. He is a mighty nice fellow. Most all the boys here are old Tours men and they speak most gratefully of what you did for them, and how much you meant to them while they were at Tours. There is so much noise going on in this tent that I cannot keep my mind on this letter. Most of our boys come down with bad motors and are taken prisoners, so if I suddenly disappear, the chances are I am a prisoner. Just remember that and it will save you a lot of unnecessary worry.

This is a pretty comfortable little camp, though not quite as good as the last one. We are living in tents with stoves to keep us warm. The furniture is mostly captured from the Germans and the music is furnished by the continuous booming of the guns on the front. Some of the old boys of our squadron are here and a lot of fellows I used to know at Issoudun. We have a mighty congenial bunch, so it is all cream. Please write when you get time. Lots of love, Percival

Wednesday, October 2: The 27th was scheduled for the early patrol this morning but it was too foggy to get off. Colton* and Stuart* got off early on a balloon straffing expedition but both got lost when the fog came in. Colton landed well south but Stuart tried to land, zoomed some trees, hit a telegraph line, and crashed. Fortunately he only cut his nose. In the afternoon Rucker*, my flight leader, took me up around Verdun to show me some of the landmarks around here so that I could find my way if I got lost. It was mighty interesting to see that poor old town all blown to pieces but still holding strong. It was surrounded on all sides by forts which command the entire country. The old lines around the town in a horseshoe [shape] are still plain to be seen. As we flew down low a couple of the long range guns opened up. Though I could not hear a sound I could see the flash and the smoke as the old gun jumped back. We got back late but there was nothing else going on.

Thursday, October 3: Well I got on my first regular patrol over the lines this morning and I must say it was mighty interesting. As we came up to the lines I could see the guns flashing in long strings across the country. There seemed to be thousands of them shooting almost constantly. Way off to the other side the shells were falling with little puffs of smoke. The ground all around was torn up with shell holes, trenches, and barbed wire. It was so mixed up I could not tell for the life of me which were our trenches and which belonged to the enemy. We passed over a couple of miles of torn up ground, wrecked roads and blown up trucks, villages leveled to the ground, and forests mowed low.

I thought we must be pretty well into Germany when crack, bang, crash and my old plane jumped and twisted around as if it had a fit. I looked around for the Archie [anti-aircraft fire] puffs but there were none to be seen. Crack, jerk and something else went by. At last I figured out what it was. We were flying in the trajectory of our batteries and the shells were passing us close enough to shake our planes. I was just thinking of the old saying, "you never hear the shell that hits you," when something else took place to draw my attention. Over to our right the Archie was bursting in long lines of black puffs. It was mighty interesting to see the stuff form something out of nothing. Thud! Thud! Whang! and three shells burst so close I could almost smell the smoke. I don't know what my plane did or what I did to it, but when I got her leveled out I was somewhat lower and well to one side. They say Archie isn't dangerous but I disagree. I heard of a fellow who got killed by some of that stuff.

The leader eased down over what I thought were some of our trucks. I was just looking them over when I saw a fellow swing up a machine gun and let fire right at us. Up came those blamed incendiary, explosive, and tracer bullets hissing and smoking. Gee whiz! The leader was S-ing and twisting in a very artful way but what I pulled off made him look sick. I don't know what the gunner thought, but those Huns must have laughed to themselves.

By the time we got collected again it was time to go home so back we came. If anything, my plane was going a little better as we turned back from the lines.

I have not got a ship assigned to me yet but so far I have had pretty good luck with those I have borrowed. The time we don't actually fly we write letters, read over old dope, and ask questions. That is the main source of information. The hour for retiring is pretty early as we have not got very good lights. We live in fairly good size tents, ten to a tent with a wooden floor, two stoves, and what candles, flashlights, acetyline lights, etc., we can collect. "C" Flight is together here: Rucker*, Clapp*, Nicholson*, Rowland*, McKimmon*, Colton*, Kelton* and myself. There is an engineering officer and the adjutant with us now and then. We have a merry time.

Friday, October 4: It was a pretty poor day this morning so we did not have any patrols. It has rained so much lately that there is more mud than there is standing room. This French mud is the stickiest stuff I ever got my feet in. This afternoon it was "C" Flight's turn to take a bath. We all piled in a truck and started for Bar-le-Duc. It was quite a ride down there but the anticipation of a hot bath kept up our spirits. At last we arrived at the bath house. There were several ahead of us so we had to wait. As our turn approached we began to hear rumors that the water was not very hot. Well I should say it wasn't. McKimmon and I got a double room and before we could get washed up a bit we like to froze to death. I am off that place for life. We got home pretty late, tired, cold, and muddy (on the outside). I don't think I will take any more baths this winter. It doesn't pay. There is no use taking a chance of freezing to death.

Saturday, October 5: The mud cleared up a little bit today, so we made a couple of patrols. The early one almost proved disastrous. Nicholson was leading us and McKimmon and Colton were in the rear. As we passed under a hole in the clouds Nick saw some Fokkers above. He turned sharp to the left which threw Mac under the hole. Two Fokkers jumped on him and though he dove and maneuvered well they shot him up pretty well. He was forced to go home as his oil tank was shot. I never will forget how he expressed his feelings. When he got down he casually remarked that he thought he was shot. Sure enough he had a bullet in his right leg. That put poor old Willy Simpson McKimmon out of the fun for a while anyhow.

The afternoon patrol was more risky still. Nicholson was leading again. As we approached the lines two Fokkers dove on the two end men. Nick and I turned back on them but we did not have time to shoot before they beat it. Then Nick dropped out and I tried to get the lead twice but the others would not follow. Finally one of them followed me and we tried to find the balloon straffing expedition. It was too late however, so we patrolled. Finally he left and I found a man from the 95th and [one from] the 147th. We patrolled until eleven Fokkers got over us and five dove on us. The leader did not see them so I pulled up along side of him and waved my wings. He took one look and started for home. There was no chance for us there so we judged our work was done.

I would hate to kill all the Huns at once as there would not be any for the rest of the fellows. [Frank] Luke* has been missing for several days now and I guess he is gone for good [Fig. 19]. He went after one too many balloons. That is the most dangerous thing an Aviator can do. You dive down amid about ten machine guns, flaming onions, and fire balls. If anything hits you, you catch on fire. Or get a shot in your gas tank or something. One balloon is more creditable than two machines.

Sunday, October 6: If somebody had not told me I never would have guessed that this was Sunday. We had a rather uneventful patrol in the morning. It was quite interesting though to watch the gas shells bursting down by the edge of the woods. The town of Brieulles was all in flames. Over to the left a shell hit in an ammunition dump and up she went. Our artillery was mighty active all night and the Huns showed the results. On the afternoon patrol there were hundreds of Spads in the air. We had a time dodging them. So far this group has been doing low flying trying to catch regulage machines. We would head off every Salmson, Liberty

Fig. 19. Frank Luke and aircraft of the 27th Aero Squadron (USAF)

[DH-4], Breguet, or Hun machine we see and make him show his colors. There were some big shells landing in the woods where the gas shells were landing this morning. As they hit they exploded and showered sulphur all over. The fire started pretty soon. When we got home there was no mail, no news, and not a very good supper.

Monday, October 7: I had one long patrol this morning but outside of a few Fokkers that played around away up high nothing unusual happened. Brieulles was getting shelled pretty heavy and most of it was on fire. Over to one side a shell hit in a small munitions dump and sent it up in smoke. The afternoon patrol was for "A" Flight so I did not get in on it. I hung around in the operations office most all the day and finally went hunting to kill some time and work up an appetite for food and sleep. It is curious that I have not been able to sleep lately. I lie awake by the hour thinking what I would do under different circumstances if I were attacked by Huns. I don't think it pays to let that interfere with my sleep. Cap Rowland and Nick got a little under the weather tonight. They were awfully funny, though. They were both hopeless washouts. I don't think they will be good for much tomorrow morning on the early patrol.

Letter, October 7. Dear Frederick: The last few days have brought the most interesting and at the same time the most exciting experiences of my life. Though I have only had a taste of what fighting in the air really is, I have had enough to know that I like it and that it is as good as it is cracked up to be. The front here is mighty active so I've seen some of the best fighting there is. After being here a day or two to get used to the customs, read up some literature, talk with older men, and learn the maps, I was given a ship on the third day to fly in a patrol of older flyers over the lines. You can imagine that I was feeling pretty good as I was at last to do what I had been working and training for for the past year. I had heard the old fellows say that a new man never sees anything for the first few trips and that his only salvation is to stick close to the leader. They had told me that the Archie (anti-aircraft guns) never did any damage though they were rather nerve-wracking.

As I joined the formation at the scheduled place, I thought of the various things I had been told and determined to hear all, see all, and come back. For a while I most twisted my neck off looking around for Huns, but I soon found that though I could see plenty of machines I had no way of knowing what they were, as they were too far away. Down on the ground under us the big guns were flashing and puffing smoke. The countryside seemed to be full of them, but look as I would, I could not see the guns themselves or hear the noise. On we went, past the balloon line to our trenches. Right there was where I met our first disappointment. I expected to look down and see two definite lines of trenches filled with men shooting at each other over a space of No-Man's-Land which was filled with barbed wire, shell holes, and dead men. I thought I could just tip my plane down and shoot 15 or 20 Huns just to try out my guns. You can imagine my surprise when I looked down on just one mass of trenches, shell holes, barbed wire, and blown-up dugouts. I looked for the Boches but for the life of me I could not tell which were our lines or which were his. It was all so mixed up and torn up that I could not make head or tail out of it.

As I gazed down at the mass of torn-up ground and watched the shells bursting on each side something went rip, smash and my old plane jumped a couple of feet straight up. When I looked for the smoke there was nothing to be seen. The leader was flying along calmly in slow zig-zags with an occasional variation. Whang! something else went by with a bump. At last I figured it out. We were flying exactly in the trajectory of the batteries on both sides and their shells were going by us with a ripping of the air that jolted our planes. I looked at my altimeter and found that we were exactly at the scheduled height. There was nothing to do but take it.

Over to our left there were a lot of little round balls of black smoke about on our level. As I watched, up popped some more. "That," said I, "is Archie; I don't wonder it isn't dangerous if that is as close as they can come." It was amusing to see something appear out of nothing at all. Bang! Bang! Bang! I grabbed my stick and tried to right my plane which seemed to be as scared as a horse when someone shoots off a gun near it. The leader veered off to one side, slipped down a ways, then went on as if nothing had happened. As he did so, I saw him look around and laugh at me. I reckon he saw how scared I was.

When I looked back at the leader he had started down toward the trenches in a steep glide. We all followed him down to within a couple hundred yards of the ground when we leveled out and opened up on the trenches. Before I had time to shoot he was up again, diving, twisting, and turning like a rabbit dodging shot guns. I stayed up a little ways and watched him, sort of fascinated by his quick movements. I could see the Huns in the trenches plainly now. One swung up his machine gun and let fly. Gee whiz! It would have been all right if I had not been able to see the bullets, but here came tracers, incendiary and explosives, all spitting smoke and fire. I did some tricks that made that leader look sick. The Huns must have laughed to see me. It would not be so bad being shot at from another airplane, because if you get hit you get an honorable wound, but this getting shot from the ground! Not for mine! I am going to sit on a stove lid after this.

As we swung over toward home I hove one sigh of relief. At last I have found something that is interesting and exciting enough to suit me. Was I scared at all? Yes, I admit I was; and anybody who isn't on their first few times is either a liar or a fool. The Archie doesn't bother me much now and the shelling is nothing. I've had a couple of encounters with Huns but I have not time to write them this time. Sufficient to say that I have not hurt any of them *yet*. I am in fine health, wonderful spirits, and perfect surroundings. Love to all, Percival

Tuesday, October 8: It was rainy all the morning so we just sat around the office on duty, ready to fly if an urgent call should come in. Toward noon it cleared up a bit, and by 3:00 we were able to make the patrol. It was pretty muddy and as my ship had a light prop on it of course I had to have the hard luck to break it on the takeoff. It knocked me out of the patrol but I got the boys to fix it for tomorrow. The rest of the afternoon I spent reading dope on Aviation at the front, Hun tactics, and types of planes. Quite late in the afternoon I went hunting again but I could not find anything. I had a good walk out of it though and am pretty tired tonight.

Wednesday, October 9: I did have a day today. It was too rainy to fly this morning so I helped Kelton censor mail. It is a crime to read what some of these enlisted men write home. They get away with murder. At 3:00 we started out on the regular concentration patrol. Hoover was leading and there were five of us following him. We had not gone far before Rowland dropped out with a bad motor. Shortly afterwards Colton quit with a water leak in his machine. I then closed the V and we crossed the lines.

After about half an hour's flying over the lines my motor began to konk. She gave about six coughs and then quit. It sounded like gas trouble and sure enough I had no pressure. I tried the hand pump. No luck. Then I turned on the neurisse [choke]. Once more no luck. She would not catch. It was a cinch there was nothing to do but land so down I came. As I leveled off I saw a telegraph wire just in time to zoom it. Just ahead was a truck which I just did skim over. By that time I had no more speed and I had to set her down. As luck would have it I was right over a barbed wire entanglement with steel posts. My undercarriage hit that stuff and down I came. The wings crumpled up and the poor old machine smashed over on her back.

I pulled myself out of the wreckage without a scratch except for a little cut I got from the wire. Then I realized how lucky I had been for there was one of those steel posts sticking clear through the fuselage not two feet from where I was sitting. If that had hit me it would have "finis la guerre" for little Willy. Well I took off all the instruments and the gun amid a large crowd of French and American doughboys. A captain took me to his dugout where I telephoned home that I was all right. By that time it was six o'clock and getting dark. So I said good-by to my Artillery friends and started home.

As I was walking along a rather muddy and very dark road a big 155 let go right over my head. Gee whiz! that thing just knocked me flat. A little further on I pulled up in back of one of them and watched the boys load and fire it. I don't see how the boys stand the noise. From there I walked two kilometers down a very muddy road to Very where I was told I would have to walk two more to Cheppy. I did not have a cent of money and if I had had it I could not have got any food or a place to sleep. The whole town was blown to pieces, and there were only soldiers there. A Major Peabody of G1 gave me transportation to Rembercourt. He sure was a peach as he gave me his own Cadillac. It was a cold ride but a mighty welcome one. I got home about 11:00 all tired out.

Thursday, October 10: We had an early morning patrol this morning. That is really the best time of day to fly. As we climbed slowly up out of the air drome the red dawn was just breaking. It was beautiful to see the wings silhouetted against the dawn. By the time we got in formation it was light enough to see clearly and over we swung towards Verdun. The clouds were in two stratus. The first one was thin and the second was thick. It was pretty well fixed for a surprise attack. We eased back and forth across the line looking over all the bi-place machines that were out and passing them up one by one as they showed their colors. As we crossed the lines over three bursts of shrapnel appeared in the sky and one over towards us. It was a pretty trick but we were on to it. Just over to one side were six little Fokkers watching us three march back and forth. They did not bother us though as we kept a tight formation. After playing around for a while we came on home. There was nothing much else going on so I wrote letters and caught up on my diary.

Friday, September 11: It rained all day today so we did not have any patrols. This morning I went down to Bar-le-Duc and had a bath. This time it was somewhat warmer so we had a better time.

Sunday, October 13: It has been raining all day today. I got in a good sleep until about eight this morning but the rest of the time I just sat around the office waiting for it to clear up. At about ten o'clock word came that Germany had accepted Wilson's terms and was retreating out of France. The first may be true but they are still fighting as I heard the guns now. We discussed the possibility of going home until about dinner time and then adjourned. After dinner I wrote a couple of letters and talked war some more. Captain Grant* left me in command of the squadron and also in charge of flying till he got back. I hope he comes soon. This evening I have been writing up some of my diary and now I am going to bed before some of the drunks come in as there is a party on.

Letter, October 13. Dear Frank: So far I have been on a patrol about every day and in the meantime I have been on duty waiting to go up. As a result I have not had much time to myself. Today it is so rainy there is no chance to fly so I am going to catch up on my mail. The wonderful news that came in today about Germany's accepting President Wilson's terms and retreating all along the lines has fairly sent this camp wild. Though the war is not over yet until we have driven the Huns clear to Hun land, still it looks good for being home next spring. I had planned to be there by Christmas but that is a little early I am afraid.

The lines are advancing and it is great to fly over ground that a week ago was in the hands of the enemy, and see our artillery flashing from it. I am getting now so I can tell the difference between the gas shells, the high explosives, and the shrapnel. Yesterday they were sending over incendiary shells and it was great to see how accurate they were—in about two minutes the woods were on fire. I had a forced landing just a little short of the trenches and smashed my plane. I was not even scratched so it did not matter much except that one $11,000 plane was gone to junk.

It is a crime to see how these towns have been wrecked and the country spoiled. Some places there isn't a stone standing as high as your head. The ground is all torn up for miles around and the woods are mown down as if some great machines had cut through them. It certainly shows the four years' fighting that has been going on here. I have not heard from Russell in the past two weeks and it has been over two months since I had a letter from Alice. There are fellows coming up here from Issoudun or Tours every once in a while who bring me all the latest news from Alice and Russell. Russ is, of course, mighty anxious to come up here, but he is doing his best work where he is and I hope he will stay. I'm afraid he would be too anxious to get himself a Hun if he were here, so it is just as well for him not to come.

I am not looking for a fight. I just do my work each day and when the scrap comes I will be the better fitted for it. If I never get a Boche to my credit I will still have done my work and my duty. A man's ability is judged by the number of "successful missions" he accomplishes and not by the number of Boches he gets. If I ever get one it will be in the line of duty, not on my own hook. I am left as commander of the squadron, Officer in charge of flying, and Officer of the day all at once. So I must attend to my duties. Don't worry about me. Things are lightening up a lot and the Huns are so far back we can hardly see them any more. Lots of love to all, Percival

Monday, October 14: It was rainy this morning so I did not have to get up early. As I was Officer of the Day I did not go on any patrol but censored mail. By the time I got through the inspection it was dinner time. Land* brought me a bunch of mail and in all I got seventeen letters. We were on a patrol but it was called off. Tonight we had a time. There was a party on and I guess half the camp got drunk. I have been trying to write this while one after another came in and explained how he had been mauled in the big fight in the mess hall. From majors [probably a reference to Major Harold Hartney*] down they were all drunk but a few in our tent. Thank Heavens I don't drink and I never will touch my first drop.

Tuesday, October 15: It is still raining so our early patrol did not get off. It was just as well as most of the fellows were in pretty sad shape. At 11:30 we sent up two patrols. I was to lead one of the formations but an oil lead broke on my plane. The oil went all over everything including me. I came down and got another ship and tried to catch the formation. At Verdun this plane went bad. I landed at the advanced field and got the mechanics to look it over. There was a split in the water jacketing and a loose prop gear. They had just had dinner so I got some there. Later I tried to take my plane home but it was hopeless. I almost wrecked it in the process.

I came home in a side car through Verdun. That poor old town is all blown to pieces. Practically every building has at least one shell hole in it. I took dinner at the 185th and then got home in time for a big chicken dinner at our own mess. I don't know where I got the appetite.

Wednesday, October 16: It rained all day today. I guess the old winter of sunny France is on. We did not have any flying but sat around the fire at the operations tent and wrote letters. I got one from Alice telling of her intended trip home. I spent most of the day writing up my diary. Captain Grant came in in the evening and we all had a long talk on our boyhood tricks etc.

Letter, October 16. Dear Lucia: It has been raining so much lately that our work has been seriously interfered with. I think the French winter has set in. You know it starts early with rain, rain, rain, mud and rain. Nothing very exciting has happened to me lately, but an [account of an] ordinary patrol I had the other morning [on 10 October] might be interesting. At about 6 o'clock AM our little formation of three planes was ready to take off. We waited a few minutes for it to get a little lighter and then started off. As I climbed slowly up out of the airdrome in large circles the sky over in the east was just getting scarlet. It was beautiful to see the other two planes silhouetted against it gliding along apparently in perfect silence. I crossed over to the opposite side of the circle and joined the other two. The leader shook his wings and off he went.

The ground was mostly covered with a thick mist, but as we got over the higher ground the mist settled in the valleys. A long line of mist covered the river following it for some distance in all its curves and bends. After following it for some time we turned aside to pick up the lines. We were now over higher grounds and we could easily see the old guns flashing, and occasionally feel a jolt as a shell passed by too close. There were no other planes in the sky as I watched the effect of the artillery. There was evidently something on the hill-side that was of particular interest as the shells kept bursting and popping all over it. Over to one side a town was burning. I don't know whether we set it going or whether the Huns were moving out and left a farewell present.

Inside of an hour the joy [of the sunrise] was all gone and we could see the transports of the Huns pulling up at the roadside to await the night. One by one the roads cleared off until you would say there was not a man, truck, or mule in the country. It was now broad day and the other machines began to arrive. That ended any dreamy ground-gazing and called for constant and close sky-searching. Well over in Hun-land and well above us some Fokkers were playing around, circling, diving, zooming, and turning. It is a pretty trick they have, a trap. You think they are all self-centered but every one has his eye on you. We let them play and continued our patrol.

Finally our time was up and the leader swung slowly off toward home. For a while I kept a good look-out behind but as we passed over the [lines], I sat back in my old plane, throttled her down, and considered the most efficient way to get two breakfasts when I should get home. Well it is so dark I can scarcely see if my pen is writing, so I must stop. Love to you all. Don't need to worry, as I am having a great time. Percival

Thursday, October 17: We had the early patrol this morning and as a result we had to get up at 4:30. It was so dark we could not see whether it was clear enough to fly or not. As a result we had to wait around till six before we washed out. I came back and washed, shaved, and wrote a letter to Russ before breakfast. There was nothing doing during the morning so I wrote some more letters. We had a patrol in the afternoon but shortly after we got started the clouds came down and we had to go home. One of the 147th squadron planes got loose today. It ran some distance, turned to the left and crashed. There was no one in it. [Final diary entry]

PART 8

Return to the 185th Aero Squadron; the Armistice and After, 18 October 1918 to 23 January 1919

[As suddenly as he was called into the 27th, he was called out of it, back into the 185th, as the squadron prepared to launch its first operational missions. Several important developments had occurred in the 185th during Gates' three-week absence from the unit; its mission had been changed from day pursuit to night pursuit, and it was now outfitted with Camel aircraft instead of SPADs. Gates must have known of these changes, because the 27th was located not far from the 185th; in addition, he stopped off for dinner with his old squadronmates on the 15th of October. The new mission required pilots to take off after dark and patrol the front lines, in order to be in place when and if German night bombers should attempt to cross the lines. Ground stations were supposed to detect the sound of enemy bombers and alert searchlight facilities, which in turn were supposed to signal the orbiting aircraft and pinpoint the bombers' location.

The procedures of this innovative night defense system had to be worked out through trial and error, and although the pilots of the squadron adapted quickly to the new system, the war ended before it could be fully implemented. The greatest challenge facing the pilots was the development of their night flying proficiency, for until this time, pursuit patrols had been flown exclusively during daylight hours. An additional challenge was presented by the fact that the airfields were not equipped with lights, and airfield landing areas had to be marked with flares, fires, or vehicle headlights. Nor were the aircraft equipped with landing lights, and efforts to attach fixed flares or utilize parachute flares were not completely successful.

His most harrowing experience with the 185th was a night crash-landing in a Camel after his aircraft ran out of fuel. According to the squadron records, this accident occurred on the second night of operational flying, on the 22nd of October, when Gates flew his first operational night flight. Fortunately Gates was not hurt; a fellow pilot in the squadron, Lt. Ewing, was killed in a night landing on the 28th of October.

In addition to his night forced landing, the other major event of his stay in the 185th in the final three and a half weeks of the war was the disappearance of his friend, Lt. E. H. Kelton. Kelton had accompanied him on his temporary assignment to the 27th and returned with him to the 185th. On the 30th of October, Kelton and Gates were tasked to undertake an afternoon balloon straffing patrol; Gates' engine malfunctioned, however, and he was forced to return and land. Kelton never returned from the mission.

Gates and a friend made a trip to the front lines on the 11th of November, apparently in the hopes of learning something about Kelton's fate, but their trip was fruitless. On the 19th of November, Gates packed Kelton's personal effects for shipment home. Unknown to Gates, Kelton had been shot down and taken prisoner by the Germans, and on the 20th of November, the day after Gates shipped Kelton's personal effects home, Kelton made his escape from the prison at Landsruhe, Germany, by walking out, eventually returning to France via Strasbourg.

The routine of combat flying in the 185th was interrupted frequently by rainy weather in late October and early November. In the week before the armistice Gates was primarily occupied with supervising the training of new pilots in the operation of the Camel aircraft. Because it was a single-seat aircraft, Gates would have coached his students and watched their performance from the ground; he himself did little flying, according to his letters. One other pleasant interruption occurred during this period: from the 25th through the 27th of October he was allowed to travel to Tours and Paris with his brother Russell as they said goodby to their sister Alice, who was returning to the United States after completing her work with the YMCA. The armistice essentially ended Gates' flying in France, although he noted with pleasure that he had been selected as "A" Flight Commander. This appointment speaks highly of Gates' abilities, for he was still a second lieutenant, and was appointed over others of higher rank. Gates was officially released from the squadron roster on the 29th of November.

Although Gates documented relatively little of his activities with the 185th Aero Squadron after his return in October, he felt that his flying with the unit was of great importance. In a letter dated 10 January, he wrote that of all his combat flying experiences, "none of them compared . . . with the last thing, namely the 185th Night Chasse Squadron." Gates apparently made an effort to be assigned to the Army of the Rhine, the American occupation force, but was not much disappointed when his request was turned down.

After the armistice his thoughts turned more and more to seeing his family again and to planning his post-war activities. He decided to leave the army, and began to think about continuing his education. His letters home after the armistice are filled largely with accounts of spare-time activities, including a short leave in Nice and a Christmas visit to Paris. In his December and January letters home, we learn of the gradual withdrawal of the American flying forces, from the front lines, to Issoudun (where he is able to rejoin his brother Russell), to Angers, and finally to Brest, where his last letter depicts him looking westward across the Atlantic to America.]

Letter, October 29. Dear Grace: I have had a couple of exciting experiences since I spilled that plane in the barbed wire [on October

9th], but the most interesting one was when I started this new work I am now in. I have been transferred back to the old 185th Squadron which, as you know, was my original one. We are now a night flying chasse squadron. The first night I went up on a patrol [22 October], it was a beautiful clear moonlight [night]. It was a great experience to climb up in the air with just the stars and moon above and the dark, black earth below. As I flew back and forth along the lines I tried to figure out where I was and how I could dissuade our own searchlights from picking me up and shooting at me. It did not make much difference as they never came very close. After a while they got tired and quit of their own accord. I sailed along peacefully, climbing and gliding, turning, floating. It was beautiful up there all alone in the moonlight.

Suddenly my engine began to miss and then quit altogether. It was out of gas on the main tank. I turned on the auxiliary. It ran by fits and starts but not enough to maintain my altitude. Hence I started as best I could determine to keep up as long as possible. As she came down I looked for a place to land. There were roads and dark patches I took for woods but that was all I could see. Ah! at last there were some white hangars. I pulled the string to release my big parachute flare which should light up the country for about two miles around. The old thing fell to earth without opening. Slowly I glided down as close as I could figure in the dark; as I leveled off I lit one wing landing flare. That showed up the ground around me but not that [ground] in front.

The wheels touched the ground and then something happened. I am not just sure what, but I found the plane upside down, with me still in the seat. That did not worry me any as I had been that way before, but I could not get out as the cockpit was flat with the ground. It was only a minute, however, till some fellows lifted up the machine and I crawled out, sick at heart to see my brand new plane all smashed to bits. As usual, I did not even get a scratch. Since then I have been flying a good deal at night, but nothing exciting has happened.

Russ came up to see me the other day so that he could make a first hand report to Alice before she went home. I think he had a good time up here and the little change did him good. He was pretty well tired out and needed the rest. Well fortunately, when the C.O. heard that Alice was going home, he let me off for three days to see her. Russ and I went down together to Paris and then I went on to Tours. I had a mighty good time and of course was glad to see her before she went home. Now I am back at work again and glad to be here. By what the papers say I judge the old war won't last long now. Well, we are quitting for the night, so I guess I'd better close this letter. Love to all, Percival

Letter, November 4. Dear Father: In case of accident you should write to [the Quartermaster General] and either have him take the remainder of the payment out of my "six months pay," which the government gives after the death of an officer, or else have him send back the money I have already paid with interest. All that of course is in case of accident. I am bringing up all these things because we have so much trouble with other fellows' stuff if they go missing as they sometimes do.

As to my personal belongings, according to AEF regulations backed up by the 1st Pursuit Group, all belongings of a man who is missing in action for over 10 days are packed up and sent to the "effects depot." There, everything except the most personal things, such as watches, picture albums, diaries, letters, jewelry etc, are sold or thrown away and the proceeds are sent home. Since this is the case, we have a custom here of selling everything except the personal things to fellows here in the group, such as blankets, bedding rolls, cots, leather goods, and toilet articles. However if the goods is claimed from the "effects depot" by a member of the family, it is given over intact.

I tell you this and I am writing the same to Russell so that you will understand the red tape that has to be gone through. This is purely a business letter; I will try to write a more interesting one to Mother a little later. Don't think I am in any special danger. I am merely getting things straightened out that I should have attended to long ago. Your loving son, Percival

Letter, November 11. Dear Mother: This is probably to be the greatest day in the World's History. For this morning at 11:00 for the first time in over four years all the noise, guns, and fighting at the front stopped. Up to the last few minutes there was a great roar of artillery fire as if everybody was trying to get rid of all his ammunition. Then suddenly all the noise stopped and a great shout rose from all over the camp. The 11th hour of the 11th day of the 11th month will never be forgotten. We are, of course, carrying on as before, but we do not make any hostile patrols. We can fly if we wish but we do not have to fly, except very little, to keep in practice.

Yesterday another fellow and I went on a motorcycle trip toward the lines to look up a fellow who is missing [Kelton]. We had so much tire trouble we had to turn around and come back. However we did not get far before we had to turn in and stay at a Military Police Headquarters overnight and we had only two blankets between us that one of the men loaned us for the night. We started in with plenty of determination, but at 10:00 we absolutely froze out. There was only one other place to go so we went there. It was the Captain's office and there was a stove there with plenty of wood. A fellow had to stay up in the office all night, so we stayed with him. It was a lucky thing we did as it went a good deal below freezing during the night. There was very little sleeping, but plenty of heat. After getting breakfast with the enlisted men, we spent about two hours roaming over an old battlefield collecting souvenirs. Then we fixed our tires and went home. I certainly am glad I have a nice warm place to live in with plenty to eat and a good bed to sleep in. I must stop now and write to Russell. Love to all, Percival

Letter, November 14. Dear Auntie: We have to fly every once in a while to keep our hand in. But no more night flying. It was pretty good fun when there was a good moon but on dark black nights it wasn't much fun. The principal thing now is, "When are we going home?" There are so many rumors around here that it is impossible to draw any definite conclusions. We may go with the Army of Occupation to the Rhine and stay there until everything is over, or else we may go home with the first bunch. We will probably know within a week or two what is to become of us.

Though I am still a second lieutenant with no prospect of a

raise in rank I have been promoted in position. I am now a Flight Commander. That does not amount to much now that the war is over, but nevertheless it is quite a raise. There are three of them to a squadron. We now have a new Commanding Officer [Captain Jerry Vasconcells*] who is a peach [Fig. 20]. The other was too, but he was not quite so good a C.O. The French have been celebrating in great style. Two days ago I visited Nancy on a trip for some ships. There were about 2000 people in the main square who all started off in a parade behind five bands and a torch light procession. The French seem to think that the only way to celebrate is to drink up everything in town. You can imagine what a mess it turned into. The fellow I was with and I went to bed pretty early to avoid trouble. There is a tremendous difference between the feeling of the French two weeks ago and the French now. You can imagine what a great relief it is to them. Love to all, Percival

Letter, November 20. Dear Old Fred: Alice must be home by now and she has told you almost everything that has happened in France since she arrived. After I saw her [before she left France] I came back here and found that my squadron was about out of commission awaiting replacements. I was given the job of training the new fellows on the Camels we use. As a result I did not get much flying myself.

I went up one afternoon [30 October] with a very good friend of mine [Lt. Kelton] to strafe balloons. My motor broke down smashing one piston just as we crossed the lines. I managed to get home, losing altitude as I went, but landed safely. The fellow I went with never came back. I packed up his effects yesterday and officially gave him up as lost. That little busted engine probably saved me from whatever happened to poor old Kelton. Thank Heaven I have no regrets. If I did not get a Hun machine or balloon I got through and that is more than some of the others did. I never missed a patrol and I never hesitated to volunteer when volunteers were called for. Now, however, I am through. I fly when I have to, but not otherwise. As a result, I get up about every third day for a few minutes. We are due to move south a ways in a few days. We will probably go to Bar-sur-Aube. We don't know a thing beyond

Fig. 20. Capt Jerry Vasconcells and aircraft of the 185th Aero Squadron (USAF)

that. I volunteered to go to the Rhine with the Army of Occupation but I guess I am not needed as I was not called. It would have delayed my home-coming a little but I figured that the experience would have been worth it. Love to all, Percival

Letter, November 22. Dear Frank: Just six months ago today I sailed out of old New York and said good-by to God's country. Only six months ago, and it seems like six years. Now that everything is over and we are just waiting around it is pretty hard to find enough to do to keep busy. I spend most of my time hunting, though I never get anything and usually only have rocks to throw if I should happen to see a bird or rabbit. The combination of plenty of food, exercise, and sleep is making me so fat that my clothes hardly fit any more.

There is very little flying these days as we are painting up our ships and getting them ready to turn in at any time we get orders to move. Here is a takeoff on the 23rd Psalm:

1. The Camel is my ship, I shall not want another.
2. It maketh me to "panne" in rough shell-holes and land by swampy rivers.
3. It tormenteth my soul; it leadeth me astray on cross-countrys.
4. Yea when I fly o'er the lines of the enemy I fear much evil, for it is treacherous; its guns and its engine, they worry me.
5. It preparest a crash before me in the land of my enemies, it covereth me with oil, the tanks leaketh badly.
6. Surely terrible night-mares shall follow me all the days of my life, and I shall live in the fear of a Camel forever.

As you see I have very little love for a Camel though they really are pretty good ships. I have crashed two of them, as I told you, one in the ocean and one doing night flying. I think I can run the rascals now, though.

We are still at Rembercourt and as they have taken away all of our transportation there is not much prospect of moving very soon. We have good warm quarters here though so there is no hurry about moving out until we can go to the port of embarkation. I have been doing my week's washing this evening. Love to all, Percival

Letter, November 24. Dear Father: We have had no orders yet to move and the general opinion seems to be that we will be here for a month or two yet before we think of going home. I believe we will not do anything definite till the peace terms are signed. In the meantime I spend my time getting enough exercise to digest the enormous quantities of food I consume each day. I went hunting this afternoon with an army rifle. It was rather a deadly weapon to use on birds and rabbits, but it worked pretty well as I killed one rabbit and scared two others rather badly. If I do as well each day we will have quite a Thanksgiving dinner. The country around here is fine for hunting, but we have no dogs and only one shotgun, so we don't have much luck. A rifle is too long range to do much shooting.

I have had a couple of letters from Russell lately and he seems to be doing finely, though he does hate his job. I suppose Alice has been home some time and has got quite civilized again. It certainly will seem funny to me to live in a real house and eat at a regular table and sleep in a soft bed, and best of all be able to go where I like without asking permission and having to be back by a certain minute. I am afraid you will find me pretty restless when I get home. This out of doors life has got me. It is so dim by this candle that you will have a job reading what I have written so I won't bother you any more. Your loving son, Percival

Letter, December 6. Dear Alice: I am sure you must be home by now and that by the time this letter reaches you you will be pretty well settled down. As Russell has already written you, I am here [at Issoudun] with him. All of the old men of each squadron were sent down here to take a physical examination and go home. I have had my exam and am waiting orders to go home. It will take two or three weeks for them to come through and then there ought not to be much more delay. Merry Christmas and lots of love to you all. Percival

Letter, December 17. Dear Lucia: I have just come back from a seven days' leave of which I spent four days at Nice in southern France. It took twenty-four hours to get to Nice but it certainly was worth the trip when I once got there. I got fixed up in a very nice little hotel that was both reasonable and comfortable. Though there were a great many Americans there, there were enough hotels so that it was not too crowded. The first afternoon I took a beautiful drive around the city and some of the surrounding country. The whole place is full of the most beautiful villas and gardens I ever saw, all looking out on the wonderful deep blue Mediterranean.

One day four of us took a tram ride up to Monte Carlo. That sounds pretty bad, doesn't it! But we went through curiosity only. The AEF is not allowed in the casino during gambling hours. We went through the place before they started, however, and saw what is probably the greatest gambling house in the world. Outside of that the grounds and buildings are perfectly beautiful. Everything looks out over the sea from a high plateau coming out of the side of a mountain. The gardens are very beautiful and the great mountains behind are perfectly wonderful. From Monte Carlo we went on up to Menton over a winding trolley line that was built into the side of the mountains and looked down on the beautiful little towns and sea below. Menton is just like all the other little towns along the way [but] it is the last town on the French coast and from there we walked up to the International Bridge and across the Italian border. Of course we could not go far as it was against the law to leave France, but we did get into Italy. On the way back we saw what was almost the most beautiful sight of all—sunset across the Mediterranean. I guess I must have been just in the mood for it or something, but it just won me. I don't know how I am going to settle down when I get back. I will want to see the whole United States and then start in on Europe.

In some ways a trip like that while in uniform is a great advantage. We were all in the same old American army. We all came over for the same purpose and we were all at Nice for the same reason. You could meet anybody or talk to anybody without introductions and you never need worry about having a good time.

I hope you all have had a Merry Christmas and a Happy New Year. We will help celebrate Easter perhaps. Lots of love to all, Percival

Letter, December 19. Dear Grace: I have about decided that I will spend my time reading such books as I can pick up in the Red Cross library. You know that I have never read much and that has probably handicapped me more than any other one thing. Then of course there is always plenty of time for good exercise. I eat so much that if I don't do something pretty strenuous I will be so fat that you won't recognize me. I have not heard anything more about orders. I think we will probably be here a few weeks longer. I am wondering a good deal what I will do when I get home, but as yet I have come to no definite conclusion. Love to all of you dear ones, Percival

Letter, December 21. Dear Father: There is not much doubt but that we will be over here for a month or two yet as the army is wholly incapable of taking care of the problem of getting us home. The ports are so jammed with men that the authorities don't know where they are at. There will be nothing accomplished until they get things straightened out and work out a system. Russ and I are managing to keep pretty busy and contented. At least you have no need of worrying about us. We are in no physical danger, having finished flying, and we keep busy enough to keep us out of trouble.

I've been wondering a good deal what I will do after I get back from France. Of course there will be a general relaxation for a few months, but what after that? It is at least mighty interesting to think about it and plan some. There is one thing I am pretty certain about. That is that I am not going to stay in the army. I would be glad to volunteer again when it is necessary, but I am not going to sponge on the government for a living. Sam has just come back from a little leave and we are going over to Russell's room to plan some kind of a Christmas party. I can hardly realize that this is the 21st with only four more days before the celebration of the greatest Christmas in four years. Well this may reach you by New Year's so a Happy New Year to you all. Lots of love, Percival

Letter, December 23. Dear Mother: This morning I managed to get my eyes open at about eight o'clock after a very heavy sleep, the after-effect of a vapor bath which Sam, Russ and I indulged in last night. Due to the bath the night before, washing was more of a formality than a necessity, which considering the icy temperature of the water might easily be dispensed with. A little hairbrushing was necessary however in order to make an orderly appearance at the French breakfast of coffee or chocolate, bread and jam served at the Red Cross.

We moved out through the crowd into the rain and mud, for which this place is famous. There was another long line on the Quartermaster's window, but we stuck it out in high anticipation of a big celebration and possibly a little party of toast, cheese, sardines, and chocolate candy. On the side wall was a large sign intended to discourage the less wily and determined members of the camp. It read:

> Today's list of sales—*No* shaving soap. *No* shoe brushes. *No* gum. *No* chocolate. *No* canned peaches. *No* crackers. *No* cigarettes. *No* cigars. *No* sales before 10:30.

It was only a bluff and we knew it. That's why we waited and our patience was rewarded by a box of candy apiece and some sardines.

There was a good fire in my stove opposite my bunk and the usual meeting of the "old ladies' club" was going on. Harry Harkins* was displaying a new pair of light Bedford cord breeches that he was trying to sell for enough to finance a trip to Paris, while Wardwell* and Hall were diligently polishing shoes, leggings, and belts in prospect of a similar trip. Two other fellows were bidding against each other for the breeches but it was apparent that they did not half appreciate the quality of the article or the present price of "real English Bedford cord." I got out a needle and thread and started sewing on a service stripe.

Finally I got through with my sewing and started for the mess hall of the Red Cross. Sam met me as per schedule and we ate together. It was a pretty good meal—hash, potatoes, peas, brussels sprouts, chocolate or coffee, and chocolate pudding for dessert. My appetite took care of it as usual. I am getting worried for fear I will get too fat before I get home. A promise to go souvenir hunting took Russ off for the rest of the afternoon so I retired to the Red Cross reading room and once more took up Conan Doyle's "The Refugees." I have been reading a good deal lately and I think it is going to be a fine way to kill the time between now and home. About 4:00 I went over to get the afternoon's mail. It was a great success. There were three letters from home, two from Ft. Worth, and a Christmas card from Atlanta. The letters from home were what started me writing this foolish thing which has gone plenty far enough. Though I attended "tea" here this afternoon, I once more feel the pangs of hunger and I must go to supper. Movies tonight will end a happy and contented day, which followed by a fine sleep keeps me in good shape and spirits. Lots of love to all, Percival

Letter, December 28. Dear Auntie: The first Christmas that I ever spent away from home passed very successfully. Russell, Sam, and I got a three days' pass and went up to Paris. I've been there several times but always just passing through so I had really never seen much of the city. This time, however, we had a fine chance to see a little and get some idea of the place. The stores are the most wonderful I have ever seen. I would hate to trust myself with a lot of money, for fear I would buy out the town. As it was, we were contented to look at the things and pass on.

Christmas morning we decided we would have to have a big dinner, and yet we did not want to go to some large place and have to pay about three times what the dinner would be worth. So we went to a little restaurant and put in an order. They did not have a thing we wanted but they thought they could get it. We lent a lot of cake chocolate to be made into some hot chocolate and told them that we would return in an hour. Well, they had the nicest little meal you ever saw for us when we came back. Chicken (roasted whole), french fried potatoes, some kind of vegetable around the side, white bread, butter, jam, brussels sprouts, chocolates, green peas, and a dessert of cut up fruit. It was really an awfully good meal. The weather is as poor as usual—rain and mud—but it is not cold and as yet we've had no snow, so it is not as bad as it might be. We are indoors most of the time, so everything is all right. Well my pen is getting low in ink so I'd better stop. Lots of love to all, Percival

Letter, January 5, 1919. Dear Frederick: On the 1st of January I got a beautiful New Years' present of my orders to Angers which is the second stop towards home. The first was when I was ordered to Issoudun. Now Russ, Sam Moonan, Manley, and I are all together here at Angers where we await orders to a base port. When those orders come through we will be pretty close to the final step. It will be from three weeks to a month before we get out of here. Then we will be held up probably a week at the base port. Angers is quite a nice little town from what I could see of it coming through. There are some pretty good stores and old castles.

We are living out at a new French caserne which has been taken over by the Americans as a Casual Officers' Concentration Camp. A French caserne is a combination of barracks and drill ground for the stationing and training of permanent standing troops. Almost every city of any size has at least one such place. The Americans use all the large stone barracks and also a lot of little wooden barracks that they have put up on the drill ground. It is quite a comfortable place and I think we can get everything fixed up very nicely in the time we will be here. There is always plenty of writing and reading to do. We will probably be on the water before any more letters can reach us. Yours with love, Percival

Letter, January 9. Dear Franklin: Russ and I are still here at Angers waiting our orders to a base port. It looks as if it would be well into February before they come through and then we will have quite a little wait at the port before sailing. So now the best we can hope for is some time in March. The men are coming in here and other places so fast that everything is clogged up. Also we hear that they have had some hard luck about getting the boats over here. As you know, the *Great Northern* went on the rocks (sand bar) and the *Leviathan* was out of order for some time. All such things hold us up. However Angers is a very interesting old town and there is plenty to do here to keep us busy. Lots of love to you all, Percival

Letter, January 10. Dear Cousin Helen: The main item of news with me is that I am still alive and pulling hard for home. I was with the 27th Aero Squadron for about a month—the last of September and the first of October. We were in the 1st Pursuit Group on the Argonne-Verdun sector. It was great work on a pretty lively sector, but as I was just starting in I did not get an opportunity to get any Boches. Like many others I came out "fifty-fifty" with them. Though I did not get any I had some experiences I wouldn't take anything for. We had a fine squadron and the work was wonderfully interesting and exciting.

None of them compared, however, with the last thing, namely the 185th Night Chasse Squadron. I had never flown at night and knew nothing of the work. However no one else did either, so we all started off square. The idea was to patrol the lines at night and keep the Huns from sending over bombing planes. We were to have the aid of search-lights on the ground which would concentrate on the Boche plane. Then we were to attack it. That was a fine system, but it required a pilot trained in night flying, a well-equipped machine, numerous landing fields, and perfect co-operation with the search-lights. We started in work lacking all these things, but we had enough pep to take us over the hard part at the start.

The first night another fellow and I were sent up on a two hours' patrol. It was our first trip at night and was naturally pretty interesting. Down below you could see the guns flashing with long red spurts of fire; on over the other side the shells were bursting with little short flashes. Now and then the ground would be all lit up by a big star shell, and then you could see the little spits of fire from the rifles as they shot at the target shown up by the light. There was nothing in the sky as far as I could see except the occasional beam of a searchlight that flashed a challenge at me. It was a wonderful feeling to be up there alone in the pitch black night as sort of a combination of nervous excitement and pleasure.

Finally my engine began to miss. I could tell by the way it acted that I was about out of gasoline. As I looked down and tried to distinguish the woods from the open ground, I confess I was somewhat worried. My altimeter registered 6000 feet but there was not a sign of a landing field. The airdrome was twenty miles away. For six miles back of the lines the ground was impossible for landing on account of the shell holes and barbed wire. I aimed my machine toward home and glided as flat as I could. At 3000 feet I dropped my only "parachute flare." It was supposed to light up the country so that I could pick out a field, and then make some kind of a landing. My luck was against me. The flare did not work and dropped without lighting.

As I neared the ground I made out the white hangars of an airdrome. Though I could not see the ground I decided to land on that field so that help would be close at hand. It was lucky that I did. When I thought I was close to the ground, I lighted my wing flares which are attached to the tip of each wing. It did not do any good and the next thing I knew there was a crash and an awful bump, and I found myself upside down, but still strapped in the seat. I undid the buckle and tried to get out. No luck! The top wing had been smashed off and the fuselage was flat to the ground leaving no way out; I was pinned under. Through a little crack I could see my flares still burning on the ends of my wings. It was only a question of minutes before the flares would set the wings afire, and the wings the gas tank etc. I don't hesitate to admit that I was scared to death.

However this time I was more lucky. Some men had seen me come down and rushed out to help me, getting there not a minute too soon. That was my first night patrol. The other fellow had no better luck. He crashed about fifteen miles from the field. The fact is, they sent us on a two hour patrol when we only had gas for an hour and a half. That was only the first of several exciting trips that I had at night but it may give you some idea of what we were doing.

Russ and I are together now at Angers awaiting orders to a base port. We expect to get home about the 1st of March. I hope we will be able to get down as far as Fort Worth on our expected auto trip. At least we will probably see you next summer. Lots of love to you all, Percival

Letter, January 12. Dear Old Al: I have not heard a word from you since I saw you last at Tours on my little visit before you left. However from what the family says, you are too busy to write so I will excuse it. It must be great to see the old place and everybody again. Russ and I will have that sport soon, I hope. "Soon" means within a month or two. They are sending men out regularly here, though not in as big numbers as they are coming in. We will be coming along in a few weeks, though. They take the Class B, C, and D men first, of course, so that delays us somewhat. However, Russ, Sam, and I keep pretty busy writing and reading. There is also a good deal of pretty interesting country around here. Lots of love, Percival

Letter, January 14. Dear Lucia: We are still waiting around here at Angers. There is no sign of orders for us and no prospect of them for some time yet. I think the first part of March is a fairly close guess. I have about decided that it is high time I was beginning to educate myself since I am out one college education. As a result I am reading any good books I can get hold of. I think I will start with history, as that subject is most interesting just now. I am now halfway through a short history of America which recalls the course in I took in American history at Hill [School]. I think I will probaby take up French history next. Outside of my reading I am doing considerable letter writing.

Alex Stevenson came in to Camp the other day. He is also awaiting orders home. Poor old Alex, his little plan did not work out. As Alice has probably told you, Alex and June Roberts tried to get me to take a job at Orly with them. Alex put in my name, without letting me know about it. Fortunately I just found it out in time. It would have kept me from going to the front, and as Alex said, "he would have done our family a great service." His idea of Service and mine are quite different. Otherwise he would never have worked so hard to get the job he did. It makes me sore every time I think of it. Well it is getting towards noon and I must go after something to eat. Lots of love, Percival

Letter, January 20. Dear Grace: Russ, Sam, and I have accomplished our third step in our slow march home. We are now all together at Brest awaiting orders and a ship. There is nothing in sight at present and it will be from ten days to two weeks before we can expect to get started. We are living in a rather crude camp just outside the city in a part of the old fortifications. Alice may know where it is—"Port de Foye." The barracks are only temporary affairs but the beds are comfortable and the food is fair. Besides, we could stand anything finely, when we are so near home. They let us out of camp now and then so we get a little look around at the country. Of course, I have been here before so I have a little idea of what is interesting.

We had a pretty good entertainment last night by some of the Y entertainment circuit. They certainly have given a lot of amusement and pleasure over here. I think it helps almost more than anything else at times.

We sent you a Cablegram this morning saying "All together. Well. Sailing indefinite." You will get it long before this letter reaches you. It has been quite a while since we have heard from you as our mail is now being sent back home again. Save our letters, as we will want to have some when we get there. This is interesting here as we can see what boats come in the harbor and go out, and we know our turn is coming. Lots of love, Percival

Letter, January 23. Dear Lucia: This is just a note as I sit in the YMCA chocolate shop at Brest waiting for my drink to cool off a bit. Russ and Sam are reading across the table. There is no dope on sailing yet except that it will be quite a while yet. The boats all seem to get loaded up in England so by the time they get to Brest there is only room for six to ten officers. There are several hundred ahead of us so you can see how we are held up. There are quite a few beautiful and interesting places around here though, so we are having a good time.

This morning the sun actually came out, so we took a little walk. There was a very beautiful old place over on a hill that we went all over. The old Chateau looked out over the bay and harbor as far as you could see. Well the chocolate is cool so that Russ and Sam are getting it all, including my crackers. I must stop. Lots of love, Percival

[Percival Gates and his brother Russell sailed from Brest on Sunday, 26 January, on board the *S. S. Cedric*. They arrived in New York on the 4th of February and were discharged from service on the 7th of February, 1919. In a little over thirteen months he had received his training as a pilot, flown in combat in France, and voyaged to and from Europe. In spite of the fact that he had never directly attacked a German aircraft, he had good reason to feel that he had done his part in ending the war.

He was fortunate to have survived the war, for he had been involved in a number of major aircraft accidents and incidents, any one of which could have resulted in injury or death. In his 1918 flying career, in training and in combat, he experienced eight forced landings, three of which resulted in the destruction of the aircraft (two in Sopwith Camels, one in a SPAD); one ground loop in which the aircraft was destroyed (another Camel); and numerous near accidents in flight and on the ground. All of these episodes occurred while he was compiling a total flying time of between 140 and 150 hours.]

APPENDICES

APPENDIX A

P. T. Gates' Pilot's Book

Aviation Section
Signal Corps, U. S. Army

SCHOOL OR SQUADRON

Military School of Aeronautics, Georgia School of Technology—
Date Arrived: October 25, 1917   Date Departed: December 22

Primary Pilot Training, Park Field, Millington, Tennessee—
Date Arrived: January 7, 1918   Date Departed: March 15

3rd Aviation Instruction Center, Issoudun, France—
Date Arrived: June 18, 1918   Date Departed: August 1

Aviation Gunnery School, St. Jean-de-Monts, France—
Date Arrived: August 7, 1918   Date Departed: August 21

185th Aero Squadron, Colombey Airdrome, France—
Date Arrived: September 9, 1918   Date Departed: September 29

27th Aero Squadron, Colombey Airdrome—
Date Arrived: September 30, 1918   Date Departed: [no entry]

Name: Percival T Gates
Rank: Pvt 1st Class
Regiment, Corps, or Dept: School of Military Aeronautics, Atlanta
Residence: 66 South Mountain Ave, Mont Clair N.J.

APPENDIX A

Name and Address of Person to be Notified in case of emergency:
Frederick L. Gates, 66 South Mountain Ave, Mont Clair N. J.
Name and degree of relation: Father
Born in: Mont Clair N. J.
Age at enlistment: 20 yrs 8 mos
Occupation at time of enlistment: Student
Eyes: Blue
Hair: Light
Complexion: Ruddy
Height: 5 ft 7 and ⅝ in
Married or single: Single
Physical Marks: S ⅛" dia left knee cap
Place of enlistment: New York N. Y.
Nature of enlistment: A.S.S.E.R.C.
Previous military experience: None
General experience: Student
Pilot's signature: /s/ Percival T. Gates
      /s/ R. S. McNeill
        Major, Signal Corps
January 5, 1918

U. S. School of Military Aeronautics
At: Georgia School of Technology, Atlanta Ga.

Subjects		Record by Weeks								Final Exam
		1st	2nd	3rd	4th	5th	6th	7th	8th	9th	
1. Military Studies	Hours	8	8	6							
	Grade	80									80
2. Signalling	Hours	5	5	6	3	3	3	6	4		
	Grade	80	80	70	80	75	75	85			75
3. Gunnery	Hours	5	5	6	5	5	5	8	11		
	Grade	95	95	95	95	95	95	95			95
4. Aids to Flight	Hours				2	4	6	6	6		
	Grade					95	95	95			85

Flight Log

5. Airplanes	Hours	8	8	8		
	Grade	80	95	95		90
6. Engines	Hours	15	13	11		
	Grade	75	80			90
7. Aerial Obs.	Hours				13	12
	Grade				95	70

Absences: NONE
Acted as Cadet Corporal from November 27 to December 22, 1917.
Graduated: December 22, 1917

FLIGHT LOG

Date	Type of Plane	Type of Engine	Remarks	Duration (mins)	Maximum alt. (feet)
Section 1: Park Field, Tennessee					
(1918)					
1/10	JN4D	OX5	Joy ride; getting used to the air	20	800
1/10	"	"	Straight flying; getting feel of controls	20	1000
1/23	"	"	Straight flying and banking; using controls	25	800
1/24	"	"	Operating controls; taking off, banking, and landing	59	700

APPENDIX A

1/25	"	"	"	25	500
1/28	"	"	"	30	600
1/30	"	"	"	32	200
1/31	"	"	Instruction; "	3	200
2/1	"	"	"	60	200
2/4	"	"	Instruction; air work	16	1000
2/5	"	"	Instruction; taking off, banking, landing, taxying	36	300
2/11	"	"	Instruction; air work	22	800
2/13	"	"	Instruction; landings	34	300
2/15	"	"	Instruction; landings	25	400
2/15	"	"	Solo; landings	40	400
2/15	"	"	Soloing work; landings	50	400
2/16	"	"	Soloing work; landings and air work	65	2000
2/18	"	"	Soloing work; landings and eights	62	1500
2/20	"	"	"	57	2500
2/21	"	"	"	70	2000
2/22	"	"	"	75	1500
2/26	"	"	Soloing work; eights over 45°	65	2000
3/2	"	"	"	65	2000
3/5	"	"	" ; landings	85	2000

(10:40 total first solo)

Flight Log

3/6	"	"	Second soloing work; eights, landings, spirals	85	2500
3/7	"	"	" ; landing for the mark	20	200
3/7	JN4A	"	Second soloing and instruction; eights and landings	80	2000
3/8	JN4D	"	Second soloing work; eights, landings, spirals	90	300
3/9	"	"	"	70	3000
3/9	JN4A	"	Second soloing work; spirals (7:05 total second solo)	90	2000
3/9	"	"	Advanced flying instruction; stands, sideslips, spins	30	3000
3/9	"	"	Advanced flying solo; stands, sideslips, spins	30	3000
3/11	JN4D	"	Cross-country; Arlington, Memphis, Park Field	65	2000
3/11	"	"	Cross-country; Driving Park, Collerville, Park Field	100	1500
3/12	"	"	Cross-country; Covington and back	70	2000

APPENDIX A

3/13	"	"	Cross-country; Whiteville (forced landing at Summerville)	120	1000
3/14	JN4A	"	Advanced flying instruction; loops, wingovers, spins, sideslips	45	4000
3/14	"	"	Advanced flying soloing; loops, wingovers, spins, sideslips	35	4000

(Total time at Park Field 32 hrs 47 min)

Part 2: 3rd Aviation Instruction Center, Issoudun, France

Field 1

6/29	Moraine	50 HP Gnome	Rouleur work; taxying and running w/o chevalling	20	2 ft

Field 2

7/1	23m dual Nieuport Type 81	80 hp LeRhone	Dual Control instruction; taking off, flying, landing (1 hop)	14	200m
7/2	"	"	" (7 hops)	41	200m
7/3	"	"	" (3 hops)	8	200m
7/7	"	"	" (3 hops)	15	200m
7/7	"	"	Flights with the tester (3 hops)	20	200m

Field 3

7/7	23m solo Nieuport Type 80	"	Solo work; landings and takeoffs (6 hops)	60	200m

Flight Log

7/7	"	"	Solo work; air work—banking, climbing etc	30	400m
7/8	"	"	Solo work; landings and takeoffs (6 hops)	60	250m

Field 9

7/9	18m solo Nieuport Type 83	"	Solo work; landings and takeoffs (4 hops)	40	200m
7/9	"	"	Solo work; air work; eights, banks	30	600m
7/10	"	"	Solo work; landings and takeoffs (8 hops)	80	200m
7/10	"	"	Solo work; spirals	30	1500m

(Total to date: 40:15)

Field 5

7/11	15m solo Nieuport Type 24	"	Landings; landing to circle and takeoffs (15 ldgs) (B+)	105	200m
7/12	"	"	Air work; figure 8s and Ss (2 lnds) (A)	40	800m
7/13	"	"	Vrilles (2 ldgs) (A)	40	1000m
7/15	"	"	Spirals (6 ldgs) (B+)	90	1200m
7/16	"	"	Acrobacy (4 lndgs) (A+)	100	1200m

(Field 5 total 6:13)

Field 7

7/17	"	120 hp LeRhone	Landings and airwork (2 ldgs)	30	1000m

APPENDIX A

7/18	"	"	Formation flying; 2 formations; diamond formation; lead 5-place formation (2 ldgs)	180	1500m
7/18	"	"	Cross country; Romorantin and back (2 ldgs)	45	1000m
7/18	"	"	Cross country; LeBlanc and back (2 ldgs)	80	1200m
7/19	"	"	Formation flying; 3 formations; lead one; diamond point in one	360	1200m
7/20	"	"	Formation flying; 2 formations; stunt formations; lead on rt and lt turns across renversement	240	1500m
7/22	"	"	Formation flying; 1 formation; altitude formation	120	5500m
7/22	"	"	Airwork; figure eights	45	1000m

(Field 7 total: 18:20)

Field 8

7/24	Type 27?	"	Line of flight; no pictures	90	1500m
7/24	"	"	Balloons; no pictures (combat)	60	1300m
7/24	"	"	Line of flight; 7 pictures (combat)	90	1500m

Flight Log

7/25	"	"	Line of flight; 7 pictures (combat)	90	1300m
7/25	"	"	Balloon; no pictures (combat)	60	2500m
7/25	"	"	Stationary target; no pictures (left hand virages)	90	1500m
			(Total to date: 72:50)		
7/26	15m solo Nieuport Type 27	120 hp LeRhone	Line of flight; 7 pictures	90	2000m
7/26	"	"	Balloons; no pictures	60	3500m
7/26	"	"	Fixed target; 7 pictures	90	2000m
7/29	"	"	[Simulated] Combat; 7 pictures	90	2500m
7/29	"	"	"	90	2500m
7/30	"	"	Combat; 1 film (collision in air; lower wing broken)	60	2500m
7/30	"	"	Combat; 1 film	90	2500m
7/31	"	"	Combat; 1 film (forced landing, leak in gas tank)	90	2500m
7/31	"	"	Combat; no film	60	2500m
8/1	"	"	Combat; 1 film (broke rib in wing landing; elevators jammed)	90	2500m
8/1	"	"	Combat; 1 film	60	2500m
8/1	"	"	Combat; no film	90	2500m

APPENDIX A

8/3	Moraine	120 hp LeRhone	Acrobatics; trying out plane	35	2000m
8/3	Sopwith Camel	130 hp Clerget	Acrobatics; trying out plane	25	2000m

(Field 8 total: 25:00)

Aviation Gunnery School, St. Jean-de-Monts

8/12	Camel	130 hp Clerget	Trying out machine; virages and figure eights	40	1500m
8/12	Nieuport	120 hp LeRhone	Shooting on balloons; 105 shots	12	600m
8/13	Camel	130 hp Cl	Trying out machine; acrobatics	50	1500m
8/13	Nieuport	120 hp LeRhone	Shooting at balloons; 142 shots, 12 hits: 08%	34	600m
8/13	"	"	Shooting at balloons; 188 shots, 15 hits: 08%	44	600m

(Total to date: 92:50)

8/14	15m solo Nieuport Type 27	130 hp LeRhone	Shooting at balloons; 146 shots, 25 hits: 17%	37	500m
8/14	Camel	130 hp Cl	Acrobatics; everything possible including flying on back	53	1500m
8/25	"	"	"	70	1500m
8/15	Nieuport	LeRh	Shooting on silhouette; 200 shots, 106 hits: 53% v.g.	28	500m

Flight Log

8/16	Camel	130 hp C1	Acrobatics	30	1500m
8/16	"	"	Bring back from forced landing; smashed up in the ocean	4	12m
8/16	Nieuport	LeRh	Shooting on silhouettes; 200 shots, 176 hits: 88% v.g.	30	500m
8/17	"	"	Shooting on silhouettes; 200 shots, 156 hits: 78% v.g.	28	500m
8/19	"	"	Shooting on sleeve; 200 shots, 17 hits: 80%	30	1000m
8/20	"	"	Shooting on sleeve; 200 shots, 19 hits: 11%	30	1000m
8/21	"	"	Shooting on sleeve; 15 shots, lost sleeve [shot off]	10	1000m
8/22	"	"	Shooting on individual sleeve; 225 shots, 35 hits, 150%	40	1000m

(Total St. Jean 9:30)

Part 3: Ferry Pilot, Orly Field

8/28	Camel	Monosoup	Ferrying, Le Bourget to Orly	10	700m
8/29	SPAD 13	220 HS	Ferrying, Orly to Colombey-les-Belles	130	1000m
8/31	"	"	Ferrying, Venetz to Colombey-les-Belles	95	1000m

APPENDIX A

9/1	"	"	Ferrying, Orly to Venetz	55	1000m
9/2	"	"	"	40	1000m
9/3	Brequet 14A2	"	Ferrying, Orly to Colombey-les-Belles	100	1000m
9/4	Camel	Clerget	Ferrying, Juvisy to Orly	10	1000m
9/5	"	"	Ferrying, Orly to St. Jean-de-Monts	225	1000m

(Total to date: 109:55)

Part 4: 185th Aero Squadron, Colombey Airdrome

9/15	SPAD 7	180 hp Hispano	Test flight; acrobatics	50	2000m
9/16	SPAD 13	220 HS	Delivering plane to Colombey	10	1000m
9/17	SPAD 7	180 hp	Delivering plane to 185th	10	1000m
9/18	"	"	Practice flight	75	2000m
9/22	"	"	Formation	55	2000m
9/25	"	"	Formation	15	2000m
9/25	"	"	Practice	55	2000m
9/26	Camel	Mono 150	Ferrying, Venetz to Bar-le-Duc	30	1000m
9/26	SPAD 13	220 HS	"	40	1000m
9/27	SPAD 7	180 hp	Practice	75	1000m
9/28	SPAD 13	220 HS	Ferrying, Venetz to Bar-le-Duc	30	1000m
9/28	Salmson		Ferrying, Bar-le-Duc to Colombey	30	1000m
9/29	SPAD 13	220 HS	Ferrying, Colombey to Bar-le-Duc	30	1000m

Flight Log

Part 5: 27th Aero Squadron, Colombey/Rembercourt

10/1	SPAD 13	220 HS	Ferrying, Bar-le-Duc to 1st Pursuit		
10/2	"	"	Voluntary Patrol; learned country, landmarks and sector	45	6000m
10/2	"	"	Sector Patrol; no encounters	30	600m
10/3	"	"	Sector Patrol; Huns shot one man	110	600m
10/5	"	"	Sector Patrol	95	600m
10/5	"	"	Test flight; test of guns shooting at lake target	30	600m
10/6	"	"	Sector Patrols (2), attacked by Huns	185	600m
10/7	"	"	Sector Patrol	105	600m
10/7	"	"	Test flight	30	600m
10/8	"	"	Sector Patrol; broke prop taking off	05	100m
10/9	"	"	Sector Patrol; motor died, crashed in barbed wire	90	600m
10/10	"	"	Balloon Straffing [Final pilot log entry]	105	800m

List of Names

Additional information is available for some of the individuals mentioned in the narrative. The identification of the men associated with the 27th and 185th Aero Squadron is derived partly from unit records provided through the Research Division of the USAF Historical Research Center at Maxwell AFB, Alabama, and partly from other sources. Other information has been provided by the Gates family.

Bartron, Harold A. Member, 13th Aero Squadron. Died 1975.

Benson, Philip. Member, 185th Aero Squadron.

Bingham, Hiram. Commander, 3rd Aviation Instruction Center, Issoudun, from 23 August 1918 on. Previously had been Russell Gates' professor at Yale University. Later became Senator from Connecticut, actively supported aviation in America.

Brodie, Clarence A. "Steve." Later a member of the 13th Aero Squadron, killed in combat, 1 October 1918.

Brubaker, Henry J. Post-gunnery school assignment unknown.

Clapp, Kenneth S. Member, 27th Aero Squadron.

Clark, John B. Member, 185th Aero Squadron.

Colton, Samuel H. Member, 27th Aero Squadron, from Millbury MA. Profiled in *New England Aviators*.

Glendinning, Robert, Major. Later Air Service liaison officer in Italy.

APPENDIX B

Grant, Alfred A. Squadron Commander, 27th Aero Squadron, from Los Angeles CA. Died 12 July 1950.

Harkins, H. H. Member, 27th Aero Squadron.

Hartney, Harold. Commander, 1st Pursuit Group in the fall of 1918; earlier had been squadron commander of 27th Aero Squadron. Author of *Up and At 'Em*, informative and entertaining history of his experiences in France.

Hays, Frank K. Member, 13th Aero Squadron.

Hoover, W. J. Member, 27th Aero Squadron, from Raleigh NC.

Kelton, Elihu H. Member, 185th and 27th Aero Squadrons, from Palmerton PA. Profiled in *New England Aviators*, Vol I.

Land, H. L. Member, 27th Aero Squadron.

Lee, John C. Post-gunnery school assignment unknown.

Lottridge, Lois. Later married Russell Gates, 1919.

Lowe, Seth. First Squadron Commander of 185th Aero Squadron, later replaced by Capt Jerry Vasconcells.

Luke, Frank. Member, 27th Aero Squadron. Most famous pilot in unit, known as "Balloon Buster." Credited with the destruction of 14 balloons and 4 airplanes before he died on 29 September 1918; his death occurred when he attempted to shoot at German soldiers after landing in German territory. Awarded the Congressional Medal of Honor posthumously.

McKimmon, William S. Member, 27th Aero Squadron, from Raleigh NC.

Mitchell, Margaret "Peggy." Later author of *Gone With the Wind*.

Nicholson, H. W. Member, 27th Aero Squadron, from Montclair NJ.

Rowland, R. W. Member, 27th Aero Squadron.

Rucker, E. W. "C" Flight Leader, 27th Aero Squadron, from Fayette MO. Died 23 March 1945.

Slaughter, Sam. Member, 141st Aero Squadron, from Atlanta GA. Brother of Lois Lottridge's mother; Lois Lottridge later married Russell Gates.

Spatz, Carl. Commander, 3rd Aviation Instruction Center, Issoudun, during Gates' time there; was replaced by Lt Col Hiram Bingham. Flew

List of Names

with 13th Aero Squadron, September-October 1918. Spatz later changed the spelling of his last name to Spaatz to emphasize correct pronunciation ("spots," not "spats"). Later became famous as "Tooey" Spaatz, WWII General and Chief of the Air Force. Credited with three aerial victories during WWI.

Stuart, Lyall. Member, 27th Aero Squadron.

Vasconcells, Jerry C. Member, 27th Aero Sqadron; later Squadron Commander, 185th Aero Squadron, from Denver CO. Died 1950.

Wardwell, Doyen P. "B" Flight Commander, 185th Aero Squadron.

Waters, George. Member, 27th and 185th Aero Squadrons, from Pittsburgh PA.

Bibliography

Archibald, Norman. *Heaven High—Hell Deep* (Boni, 1935). Archibald, a pilot in 95th Aero Squadron, was shot down and captured.

Bingham, Hiram, Lt Col. *An Explorer in the Air Service* (Yale University Press, 1920). Contains a valuable and detailed account of air training operations at Issoudun.

Brewer, Leighton. *Riders of the Sky* (Houghton Mifflin, 1934). A poetic history of the 13th Aero Squadron, of which Brewer was a member. Brewer was credited with three victories in World War I, was later a professor of English. *Riders of the Sky* is a unique and valuable description of the U. S. Air Service effort.

Fitch, Willis. *Wings in the Night* (Marshall Jones, 1938). A good account of an Air Service pilot's training and combat experiences with the Italians.

Fosdick, Raymond B. *John D. Rockefeller, Jr.: A Portrait* (Harper, 1956). Contains numerous descriptions of the Gates-Rockefeller relationship.

[Gates, Alice.] *A Red Triangle Girl in France* (Doran, 1918). Published excerpts from letters Alice Gates wrote to her family late in 1917 and early in 1918.

Gates, Frederick Taylor. *Chapters in My Life* (The Free Press, 1977). With the Frederick Taylor Gates Lectures by Robert Swain Morison, M.D. The autobiography of Percival Taylor Gates' father, originally written in 1928, published in 1977.

Gorrell, Edgar S., Col. *The Measure of America's World War Aeronautical Effort.* Publication No. 6. Norwich University, 1940.

BIBLIOGRAPHY

Hall, James Norman. *High Adventure* (Houghton Mifflin, 1918). Hall, later a best-selling author (with Charles Nordhoff), wrote this account of his experiences as a pilot in the Lafayette Escadrille; he later flew with the 94th Aero Squadron until he was shot down and taken prisoner.

Hall, Norman S. *The Balloon Buster: Frank Luke of Arizona* (Doubleday Doran, 1928). A popular history of Frank Luke, first published in *Liberty Magazine*.

Hartney, Harold E. Lt Col. *Up and At 'Em* (Stackpole, 1940). Hartney was commander of 1st Pursuit Group while Gates was with the 185th and 27th Aero Squadrons. Hartney provides a good account of some of the 185th's night flying experiences.

Howland, Harry S., Col USA. *America in Battle* (Paris: Herbert Clarke, 1920). "With Guide to the American Battlefields in France and Belgium by Col. James A. Moss, USA." A pocket-sized reference volume giving a chronological sequence of events of the American Infantry in WWI.

Hudson, James J. *Hostile Skies: A Combat History of the American Air Service in World War I* (Syracuse University Press, 1968). Informative and well written.

Mauer Mauer, ed. *The U. S. Air Service in World War I*. 4 vols. (U. S. Government Printing Office, 1979). Valuable warehouse of Air Service documents. Vol 4 contains Harold Hartney's account of 185th night operations.

Nevins, Allan. "The Man Who Gave Away Rockefeller's Millions: The Memoirs of Frederick T. Gates." *American Heritage* 6 (April 1955): 65–86. Nevins provides an introduction to some passages excerpted from Gates' autobiography.

New England Aviators, 2 vols. (Houghton Mifflin, 1920). Vol 1 contains an account of Gates' squadronmate in the 185th Aero Squadron, Lt E. H. Kelton.

Nordhoff, Charles, and James Norman Hall. *The Lafayette Flying Corps*, 2 vols (Houghton Mifflin, 1920). An informative and entertaining summary of all Americans who flew in French flying squadrons, including the Lafayette Escadrille. Nordhoff and Hall both flew with French units before flying in American squadrons.

Presley, Curtis Edward "Cy." *Curtis Edward Presley, 1894–1975: A Pictorial Diary of World War I* (Privately printed, 1977). Presley flew with the 13th Aero Squadron. Contains many photos and documents depicting Air Service life in France in 1918–1919. Materials compiled by his daughter, Mary Martha Merritt.

Rickenbacker, Eddie, Capt. *Fighting the Flying Circus* (Stokes, 1919). An early

Bibliography

and dynamic account of Air Service combat action. Not always historically accurate.

Springs, Elliott White. *Warbirds: the Diary of an Unknown Aviator* (Doran, 1926). A robust version of training in England and combat in France, first serialized in *Liberty* magazine. Springs initially stated that this work was a diary of a friend killed in combat, John McGavock Grider. But in fact Springs was the author of all but the first few paragraphs.

Sweetser, Arthur. *The American Air Service* (Appleton, 1919). "A Record of Its Problems, Its Difficulties, Its Failures, and Its Final Achievements." An invaluable summary of Air Service work in World War I.

Thayer, Lucien H. (Lt, USAS). *America's First Eagles: The Official History of the U. S. Air Service, A. E. F. (1917–1918)* (Bender Publishing/Champlin Press, 1983). An important early history.